100
VERSES
EVERY
CHRISTIAN
NEEDS TO KNOW

The quoted ideas expressed in this book (but not Scripture verses) are not, in all cases, exact quotations, as some have been edited for clarity and brevity. In all cases, the author has attempted to maintain the speaker's original intent. In some cases, quoted material for this book was obtained from secondary sources, primarily print media. While every effort was made to ensure the accuracy of these sources, the accuracy cannot be guaranteed. For additions, deletions, corrections, or clarifications in future editions of this text, please write Freeman-Smith, LLC.

The Holy Bible, King James Version

The Holy Bible, New King James Version (NKJV) Copyright © 1982 by Thomas Nelson, Inc. Used by permission.

New Century Version®. (NCV) Copyright © 1987, 1988, 1991 by Word Publishing, a division of Thomas Nelson, Inc. All rights reserved. Used by permission.

The Holman Christian Standard Bible™ (Holman CSB) Copyright © 1999, 2000, 2001 by Holman Bible Publishers. Used by permission.

The Holy Bible, New International Version®. (NIV) Copyright © 1973, 1978, 1984 International Bible Society. Used by permission of Zondervan. All rights reserved.

The Holy Bible. New Living Translation (NLT) copyright © 1996 Tyndale Charitable Trust. Used by permission of Tyndale House Publishers.

The New American Standard Bible®, (NASB) Copyright © 1960, 1962, 1963, 1968, 1971, 1972, 1973, 1975, 1977, 1995 by The Lockman Foundation. Used by permission.

Scripture taken from The Message. (MSG) Copyright © 1993, 1994, 1995, 1996, 2000, 2001, 2002. Used by permission of NavPress Publishing Group.

Cover Design by Kim Russell / Wahoo Designs
Page Layout by Bart Dawson

ISBN 978-1-60587-111-0

100 VERSES EVERY CHRISTIAN NEEDS TO KNOW

TABLE OF CONTENTS

INTRODUCTION

The counsel of the LORD standeth for ever,
the thoughts of his heart to all generations.
Psalm 33:11 KJV

There are some Bible verses that are so important, so crucial to the Christian faith, that every believer should know them by heart. Can you focus on just 100 of these verses? Of course you can; of course you should; and this book can help.

This text examines 100 of the most familiar verses from God's Holy Word. These verses, which you've probably heard many times before, are short enough, and memorable enough, for you to place safely in your long-term mental database. So do yourself and your loved ones a favor: study each verse and do your best to place it permanently in your mind and in your heart. When you do, you'll discover that having God's Word in your heart is even better than having a Bible on your bookshelf.

VERSE 1

For God so loved the world,
that he gave his only begotten Son,
that whosoever believeth in him should not perish,
but have everlasting life.

John 3:16 KJV

THE GIFT OF ETERNAL LIFE

We begin with John 3:16, a verse that you've undoubtedly known since childhood. After all, this verse is, quite possibly, the most widely recognized sentence in the entire Bible. But even if you memorized this verse many years ago, you still need to make sure it's a verse that you can recite by heart.

John 3:16 makes this promise: If you believe in Jesus, you will live forever with Him in heaven. It's an amazing promise, and it's the cornerstone of the Christian faith.

Eternal life is not an event that begins when you die. Eternal life begins when you invite Jesus into your heart right here on earth. So it's important to remember that God's plans for you are not limited to the ups and downs of everyday life. If you've allowed Jesus to reign over your heart, you've already begun your eternal journey.

As mere mortals, our vision for the future, like our lives here on earth, is limited. God's vision is not burdened by such limitations: His plans extend throughout all eternity.

Let us praise the Creator for His priceless gift, and let us share the Good News with all who cross our paths. We return our Father's love by accepting His grace and by sharing His message and His love. When we do, we are blessed here on earth and throughout all eternity.

MORE THOUGHTS ABOUT ETERNAL LIFE

The damage done to us on this earth will never find its way into that safe city. We can relax, we can rest, and though some of us can hardly imagine it, we can prepare to feel safe and secure for all of eternity.

Bill Hybels

If you are a believer, your judgment will not determine your eternal destiny. Christ's finished work on Calvary was applied to you the moment you accepted Christ as Savior.

Beth Moore

Teach us to set our hopes on heaven, to hold firmly to the promise of eternal life, so that we can withstand the struggles and storms of this world.

Max Lucado

I can still hardly believe it. I, with shriveled, bent fingers, atrophied muscles, gnarled knees, and no feeling from the shoulders down, will one day have a new body—light, bright and clothed in righteousness—powerful and dazzling.

Joni Eareckson Tada

God has promised us abundance, peace, and eternal life. These treasures are ours for the asking; all we must do is claim them. One of the great mysteries of life is why on earth do so many of us wait so very long to lay claim to God's gifts?

Marie T. Freeman

Like a shadow declining swiftly . . . away . . . like the dew of the morning gone with the heat of the day; like the wind in the treetops, like a wave of the sea, so are our lives on earth when seen in light of eternity.

Ruth Bell Graham

A WORD TO THE WISE

God offers you life abundant and life eternal. If you have not accepted His gift, the appropriate moment to do so is now.

VERSE 2

This is the day which the LORD hath made;
we will rejoice and be glad in it.
Psalm 118:24 KJV

CELEBRATE THE GIFT OF LIFE

Today is a non-renewable resource—once it's gone, it's gone forever. Our responsibility, as thoughtful believers, is to use this day in the service of God's will and in the service of His people. When we do so, we enrich our own lives and the lives of those whom we love.

God has richly blessed us, and He wants you to rejoice in His gifts. That's why this day—and each day that follows—should be a time of prayer and celebration as we consider the Good News of God's free gift: salvation through Jesus Christ.

Oswald Chambers correctly observed, "Joy is the great note all throughout the Bible." E. Stanley Jones echoed that thought when he wrote "Christ and joy go together." But, even the most dedicated Christians can, on occasion, forget to celebrate each day for what it is: a priceless gift from God.

What do you expect from the day ahead? Are you expecting God to do wonderful things, or are you living beneath a cloud of apprehension and doubt? The familiar words of Psalm 118:24 remind us that every day is a cause for celebration. Our duty, as believers, is to rejoice in God's marvelous creation.

Today, celebrate the life that God has given you. Today, put a smile on your face, kind words on your lips, and a song in your heart. Be generous with your praise and free with your encouragement. And then, when you have celebrated life to the full, invite your friends to do likewise. After all, this is God's day, and He has given us clear instructions for its use. We are commanded to rejoice and be glad. So, with no further ado, let the celebration begin . . .

MORE THOUGHTS ABOUT JOYFUL LIVING

As Christians, we must live a day at a time. No person, no matter how wealthy or gifted, can live two days at a time. God provides for us day by day.

Warren Wiersbe

Today is mine. Tomorrow is none of my business. If I peer anxiously into the fog of the future, I will strain my spiritual eyes so that I will not see clearly what is required of me now.

Elisabeth Elliot

When the dream of our heart is one that God has planted there, a strange happiness flows into us. At that moment, all of the spiritual resources of the universe are released to help us. Our praying is then at one with the will of God and becomes a channel for the Creator's purposes for us and our world.

Catherine Marshall

When we truly walk with God throughout our day, life slowly starts to fall into place.

Bill Hybels

Submit each day to God, knowing that He is God over all your tomorrows.

Kay Arthur

Christ is the secret, the source, the substance, the center, and the circumference of all true and lasting gladness.

Mrs. Charles E. Cowman

A WORD TO THE WISE

Today is a wonderful, one-of-a-kind gift from God. Treat it that way.

VERSE 3

*In the beginning God created the heavens
and the earth. The earth was without form,
and void; and darkness was on the face of the deep.
And the Spirit of God was hovering over the face
of the waters. Then God said, "Let there be light";
and there was light.*

Genesis 1:1-3 NKJV

CELEBRATING GOD'S CREATION

In the beginning, God created everything: the things we see and the things we don't. And each morning, the sun rises upon a glorious world that is a physical manifestation of God's infinite power and His infinite love. And yet, because of the incessant demands of everyday life, we're sometimes too busy to notice.

We live in a society filled with more distractions than we can possibly count and more obligations than we can possibly meet. Is it any wonder, then, that we often overlook God's handiwork as we rush from place to place, giving scarcely a single thought to the beauty that surrounds us?

Today, take time to really observe the world around you. Take time to offer a prayer of thanks for the sky above and the beauty that lies beneath it. And take time to ponder the miracle of God's creation. The time you spend celebrating God's wonderful world is always time well spent.

No philosophical theory which I have yet come across is a radical improvement on the words of Genesis, that "in the beginning God made Heaven and Earth."

C. S. Lewis

MORE THOUGHTS ABOUT GOD'S CREATION

How awesome that the "Word" that was in the beginning, by which and through which God created everything, was—and is—a living Person with a mind, will, emotions, and intellect.

Anne Graham Lotz

God expresses His love through creation.

Charles Stanley

Man was created by God to know and love Him in a permanent, personal relationship.

Anne Graham Lotz

Because God created the Natural—invented it out of His love and artistry—it demands our reverence.

C. S. Lewis

Can't follow the stars? Follow the One who made them.

Anonymous

A WORD TO THE WISE

Every day can be a celebration of God's creation. And every day should be.

VERSE 4

After this manner therefore pray ye:
Our Father which art in heaven,
Hallowed be thy name. Thy kingdom come.
Thy will be done in earth, as it is in heaven.
Give us this day our daily bread.
And forgive us our debts, as we forgive our debtors.
And lead us not into temptation,
but deliver us from evil:
For thine is the kingdom, and the power,
and the glory, for ever. Amen

Matthew 6:9-13 KJV

THE LORD'S PRAYER

"Our Father which art in heaven, hallowed be thy name." These familiar words begin the Lord's Prayer, a prayer that you've heard on countless occasions. It's the prayer that Jesus taught His followers to pray, and it's a prayer that you probably know by heart.

You already know what the prayer says, but have you thought carefully, and in detail, about exactly what those words mean? Hopefully so. After all, this simple prayer was authored by the Savior of mankind.

Today, take the time to carefully consider each word in this beautiful passage. When you weave these Lord's Prayer into the fabric of your life, you'll soon discover that God's Word and God's Son have the power to change everything, including you.

MORE THOUGHTS ABOUT GOD

I lived with Indians who made pots out of clay which they used for cooking. Nobody was interested in the pot. Everybody was interested in what was inside. The same clay taken out of the same riverbed, always made in the same design, nothing special about it. Well, I'm a clay pot, and let me not forget it. But, the excellency of the power is of God and not us.

Elisabeth Elliot

God is not a supernatural interferer; God is the everlasting portion of his people. When a man born from above begins his new life, he meets God at every turn, hears him in every sound, sleeps at his feet, and wakes to find him there.

Oswald Chambers

God is the beyond in the midst of our life.

Dietrich Bonhoeffer

A sense of deity is inscribed on every heart.

John Calvin

God has put into each of our lives a void that cannot be filled by the world. We may leave God or put Him on hold, but He is always there, patiently waiting for us . . . to turn back to Him.

Emilie Barnes

When all else is gone, God is left, and nothing changes Him.

Hannah Whitall Smith

A WORD TO THE WISE

If you can recite the Lord's Prayer by heart, congratulations. If you can't, then what are you waiting for?

VERSE 5

The Lord is my shepherd; I shall not want.
He makes me to lie down in green pastures;
He leads me beside the still waters.
He restores my soul.

Psalm 23:1-3 NKJV

GOD'S PROTECTION

David, the author of the 23rd Psalm, realized that God was his shield, his protector, and his salvation. And if we're wise, we realize it, too. After all, God has promised to protect us, and He intends to keep His promise.

In a world filled with dangers and temptations, God is the ultimate armor. In a world filled with misleading messages, God's Word is the ultimate truth. In a world filled with more frustrations than we can count, God's Son offers the ultimate peace.

Will you accept God's peace and wear God's armor against the dangers of our world? Hopefully so—because when you do, you can live courageously, knowing that you possess the supreme protection: God's unfailing love for you.

22

The world offers no safety nets, but God does. He sent His only begotten Son to offer you the priceless gift of eternal life. And now you are challenged to return God's love by obeying His commandments and honoring His Son.

Sometimes, in the crush of everyday life, God may seem far away, but He is not. God is everywhere you have ever been and everywhere you will ever go. He is with you night and day; He knows your thoughts and your prayers. And, when you earnestly seek His protection, you will find it because He is here—always—waiting patiently for you to reach out to Him. And the next move, of course, is yours.

MORE THOUGHTS ABOUT GOD'S PROTECTION

He goes before us, follows behind us, and hems us safe inside the realm of His protection.

Beth Moore

The Lord God of heaven and earth, the Almighty Creator of all things, He who holds the universe in His hand as though it were a very little thing, He is your Shepherd, and He has charged Himself with the care and keeping of you, as a shepherd is charged with the care and keeping of His sheep.

Hannah Whitall Smith

Our responsibility is to feed from Him, to stay close to Him, to follow Him—because sheep easily go astray—so that we eternally experience the protection and companionship of our Great Shepherd the Lord Jesus Christ.

Franklin Graham

The Will of God will never take you where the Grace of God will not protect you.

Anonymous

Prayer is our pathway not only to divine protection, but also to a personal, intimate relationship with God.

Shirley Dobson

God will never let you sink under your circumstances. He always provides a safety net and His love always encircles.

Barbara Johnson

A WORD TO THE WISE

Earthly security is an illusion. Your only real security comes from the loving heart of God.

VERSE 6

*But grow in the grace and knowledge of
our Lord and Savior Jesus Christ.
To Him be the glory both now and forever.*

2 Peter 3:18 NKJV

SPIRITUAL GROWTH

The words of 2 Peter 3:18 make it clear: spiritual growth is a journey, not a destination. When it comes to your faith, God doesn't intend for you to stand still; He wants you to keep moving and growing. In fact, God's plan for you includes a lifetime of prayer, praise, and spiritual growth.

Many of life's most important lessons are painful to learn. During times of heartbreak and hardship, we must be courageous and we must be patient, knowing that in His own time, God will heal us if we invite Him into our hearts.

Spiritual growth need not take place only in times of adversity. We must seek to grow in our knowledge and love of the Lord every day that we live. In those quiet moments when we open our hearts to God, the One who made us keeps remaking us. He gives us direction, perspective, wisdom, and courage. The appropriate moment to accept those spiritual gifts is the present one.

Are you as mature as you're ever going to be? Hopefully not! When it comes to your faith, God doesn't intend for you to become "fully grown," at least not in this lifetime. In fact, God still has important lessons that He intends to teach you. So ask yourself this: what lesson is God trying to teach me today? And then go about the business of learning it.

We set our eyes on the finish line,
forgetting the past, and straining toward
the mark of spiritual maturity
and fruitfulness.

Vonette Bright

MORE THOUGHTS ABOUT SPIRITUAL GROWTH

If all struggles and sufferings were eliminated, the spirit would no more reach maturity than would the child.

Elisabeth Elliot

We look at our burdens and heavy loads, and we shrink from them. But, if we lift them and bind them about our hearts, they become wings, and on them we can rise and soar toward God.

Mrs. Charles E. Cowman

We often become mentally and spiritually barren because we're so busy.

Franklin Graham

You are either becoming more like Christ every day or you're becoming less like Him. There is no neutral position in the Lord.

Stormie Omartian

A WORD TO THE WISE

Wherever you are in your spiritual journey, it's always the right time to take another step toward God.

VERSE 7

But those who wait on the Lord
shall renew their strength; they shall mount up with
wings like eagles, they shall run and not be weary,
they shall walk and not faint.

Isaiah 40:31 NKJV

STRENGTH FROM GOD

Even the most inspired Christians can, from time to time, find themselves running on empty. The demands of daily life can drain us of our strength and rob us of the joy that is rightfully ours in Christ. When we find ourselves tired, discouraged, or worse, there is a source from which we can draw the power needed to recharge our spiritual batteries. That source is God.

God intends that His children lead joyous lives filled with abundance and peace. But sometimes, abundance and peace seem very far away. It is then that we must turn to God for renewal, and when we do, He will restore us if we allow Him to do so.

Today, like every other day, is literally brimming with possibilities. Whether we realize it or not, God is always working in us and through us; our job is to let Him do

His work without undue interference. Yet we are imperfect beings who, because of our limited vision, often resist God's will. And oftentimes, because of our stubborn insistence on squeezing too many activities into a 24-hour day, we allow ourselves to become exhausted or frustrated, or both.

Are you tired or troubled? Turn your heart toward God in prayer. Are you weak or worried? Take the time—or, more accurately, make the time—to delve deeply into God's Holy Word. Are you spiritually depleted? Call upon fellow believers to support you, and call upon Christ to renew your spirit and your life. Are you simply overwhelmed by the demands of the day? Pray for the wisdom to simplify your life. Are you exhausted? Pray for the wisdom to rest a little more and worry a little less.

When you do these things, you'll discover that the Creator of the universe stands always ready and always able to create a new sense of wonderment and joy in you.

Worry does not empty tomorrow of its sorrow;
it empties today of its strength.

Corrie ten Boom

MORE THOUGHTS ABOUT STRENGTH

No matter how heavy the burden, daily strength is given, so I expect we need not give ourselves any concern as to what the outcome will be. We must simply go forward.

Annie Armstrong

When we spend time with Christ, He supplies us with strength and encourages us in the pursuit of His ways.

Elizabeth George

The same God who empowered Samson, Gideon, and Paul seeks to empower my life and your life, because God hasn't changed.

Bill Hybels

God conquers only what we yield to Him. Yet, when He does, and when our surrender is complete, He fills us with a new strength that we could never have known by ourselves. His conquest is our victory!

Shirley Dobson

A WORD TO THE WISE

When you are tired, fearful, or discouraged, God can restore your strength.

VERSE 8

Be still, and know that I am God . . . .
Psalm 46:10 KJV

BE STILL

We live in a noisy world, a world filled with distractions, frustrations, obligations, and complications. But we must not allow our clamorous world to separate us from God's peace. Instead, we must "be still" so that we might sense the presence of God.

If we are to maintain righteous minds and compassionate hearts, we must take time each day for prayer and for meditation. We must make ourselves still in the presence of our Creator. We must quiet our minds and our hearts so that we might sense God's love, God's will, and God's Son.

Has the busy pace of life robbed you of the peace that might otherwise be yours through Jesus Christ? If so, it's time to reorder your priorities. Nothing is more important than the time you spend with your Savior. So be still and claim the inner peace that is your spiritual birthright: the peace of Jesus Christ. It is offered freely; it has been paid for in full; it is yours for the asking. So ask. And then share.

MORE THOUGHTS ABOUT QUIET TIME

The manifold rewards of a serious, consistent prayer life demonstrate clearly that time with our Lord should be our first priority.

Shirley Dobson

I don't see how any Christian can survive, let alone live life as more than a conqueror, apart from a quiet time alone with God.

Kay Arthur

Since the quiet hour spent with God is the preacher's power-house, the devil centers his attention on that source of strength.

Vance Havner

The Lord Jesus, available to people much of the time, left them, sometimes a great while before day, to go up to the hills where He could commune in solitude with His Father.

Elisabeth Elliot

In the center of a hurricane there is absolute quiet and peace. There is no safer place than in the center of the will of God.

Corrie ten Boom

When frustrations develop into problems that stress you out, the best way to cope is to stop, catch your breath, and do something for yourself, not out of selfishness, but out of wisdom.

Barbara Johnson

When we are in the presence of God, removed from distractions, we are able to hear him more clearly, and a secure environment has been established for the young and broken places in our hearts to surface.

John Eldredge

That is the source of Jeremiah's living persistence, his creative constancy. He was up before the sun, listening to God's word. Rising early, he was quiet and attentive before his Lord. Long before the yelling started, the mocking, the complaining, there was this centering, discovering, exploring time with God.

Eugene Peterson

A WORD TO THE WISE

Be still and listen to God. He has something important to say to you.

VERSE 9

And now abide faith, hope, love, these three;
but the greatest of these is love.

1 Corinthians 13:13 NKJV

THE GREATEST
OF THESE IS LOVE

The familiar words of 1st Corinthians 13 remind us of the importance of love. Faith is important, of course. So, too, is hope. But love is more important still.

Christ showed His love for us on the cross, and, as Christians, we are called upon to return Christ's love by sharing it. We are commanded (not advised, not encouraged . . . commanded!) to love one another just as Christ loved us (John 13:34). That's a tall order, but as Christians, we are obligated to follow it.

Sometimes love is easy (puppies and sleeping children come to mind), and sometimes love is hard (fallible human beings come to mind). But God's Word is clear: We are to love all our friends and neighbors, not just the lovable ones. So today, take time to spread Christ's message by word and by example. And the greatest of these is, of course, example.

More Thoughts About Love

Those who abandon ship the first time it enters a storm miss the calm beyond. And the rougher the storms weathered together, the deeper and stronger real love grows.

Ruth Bell Graham

Love is an attribute of God. To love others is evidence of a genuine faith.

Kay Arthur

He who is filled with love is filled with God Himself.

St. Augustine

Love is the seed of all hope. It is the enticement to trust, to risk, to try, and to go on.

Gloria Gaither

It is when we come to the Lord in our nothingness, our powerlessness and our helplessness that He then enables us to love in a way which, without Him, would be absolutely impossible.

Elisabeth Elliot

How much a person loves someone is obvious by how much he is willing to sacrifice for that person.

Bill Bright

Suppose that I understand the Bible. And, suppose that I am the greatest preacher who ever lived! The Apostle Paul wrote that unless I have love, "I am nothing."

Billy Graham

Carve your name on hearts, not on marble.

C. H. Spurgeon

How do you spell love? When you reach the point where the happiness, security, and development of another person is as much of a driving force to you as your own happiness, security, and development, then you have a mature love. True love is spelled G-I-V-E. It is not based on what you can get, but rooted in what you can give to the other person.

Josh McDowell

Live your lives in love, the same sort of love which Christ gives us, and which He perfectly expressed when He gave Himself as a sacrifice to God.

Corrie ten Boom

A WORD TO THE WISE

God is love, and He expects you to share His love with others.

VERSE 10

*But seek first the kingdom of God
and His righteousness,
and all these things shall be added to you.
Therefore do not worry about tomorrow,
for tomorrow will worry about its own things.
Sufficient for the day is its own trouble.*

Matthew 6:33-34 NKJV

BEYOND WORRY

Because we are imperfect human beings struggling with imperfect circumstances, we worry. Even though we, as Christians, have the assurance of salvation—even though we, as Christians, have the promise of God's love and protection—we find ourselves fretting over the inevitable frustrations of everyday life. Jesus understood our concerns when He spoke the reassuring words found in the 6th chapter of Matthew.

Where is the best place to take your worries? Take them to God. Take your troubles to Him; take your fears to Him; take your doubts to Him; take your weaknesses to Him; take your sorrows to Him . . . and leave them all there. Seek protection from the One who offers you eternal salvation; build your spiritual house upon the Rock that cannot be moved.

Perhaps you are concerned about your future, your health, or your finances. Or perhaps you are simply a "worrier" by nature. If so, make Matthew 6 a regular part of your daily Bible reading. This beautiful passage will remind you that God still sits in His heaven and you are His beloved child. Then, perhaps, you will worry a little less and trust God a little more, and that's as it should be because God is trustworthy . . . and you are protected.

The beginning of anxiety is the end of faith,
and the beginning of true faith
is the end of anxiety.

George Mueller

MORE THOUGHTS ABOUT WORRY

Worry is the senseless process of cluttering up tomorrow's opportunities with leftover problems from today.

Barbara Johnson

Never yield to gloomy anticipation. Place your hope and confidence in God. He has no record of failure.

Mrs. Charles E. Cowman

We are not called to be burden-bearers, but cross-bearers and light-bearers. We must cast our burdens on the Lord.

Corrie ten Boom

This life of faith, then, consists in just this—being a child in the Father's house. Let the ways of childish confidence and freedom from care, which so please you and win your heart when you observe your own little ones, teach you what you should be in your attitude toward God.

Hannah Whitall Smith

A WORD TO THE WISE

Work hard, pray harder, and if you have any worries, take them to God—and leave them there.

VERSE 11

Trust in the Lord with all your heart,
and lean not on your own understanding;
In all your ways acknowledge Him,
and He shall direct your paths.

Proverbs 3:5-6 NKJV

TRUST HIM

It's easy to talk about trusting God, but when it comes to actually trusting Him, that's considerably harder. Why? Because genuine trust in God requires more than words; it requires a willingness to follow God's lead and a willingness to obey His commandments. (These, by the way, are not easy things to do.)

Have you spent more time talking about Christ than walking in His footsteps? If so, God wants to have a little chat with you. And, if you're unwilling to talk to Him, He may take other actions in order to grab your attention.

Thankfully, whenever you're willing to talk with God, He's willing to listen. And, the instant that you decide to place Him squarely in the center of your life, He will respond to that decision with blessings that are too unexpected to predict and too numerous to count.

The next time you find your courage tested to the limit, lean upon God's promises. Trust His Son. Remember that God is always near and that He is your protector and your deliverer. When you are worried, anxious, or afraid, call upon Him. God can handle your troubles infinitely better than you can, so turn them over to Him. Remember that God rules both mountaintops and valleys—with limitless wisdom and love—now and forever.

MORE THOUGHTS ABOUT TRUSTING GOD

Sometimes the very essence of faith is trusting God in the midst of things He knows good and well we cannot comprehend.

Beth Moore

A prayerful heart and an obedient heart will learn, very slowly and not without sorrow, to stake everything on God Himself.

Elisabeth Elliot

Brother, is your faith looking upward today? / Trust in the promise of the Savior. / Sister, is the light shining bright on your way? / Trust in the promise of thy Lord.

Fanny Crosby

God is God. He knows what he is doing. When you can't trace his hand, trust his heart.

Max Lucado

Do not be afraid, then, that if you trust, or tell others to trust, the matter will end there. Trust is only the beginning and the continual foundation. When we trust Him, the Lord works, and His work is the important part of the whole matter.

Hannah Whitall Smith

Are you serious about wanting God's guidance to become the person he wants you to be? The first step is to tell God that you know you can't manage your own life; that you need his help.

Catherine Marshall

A WORD TO THE WISE

Because God is trustworthy—and because He has made promises to you that He intends to keep—you are protected.

VERSE 12

I am the vine, you are the branches.
He who abides in Me, and I in him,
bears much fruit;
for without Me you can do nothing.

John 15:5 NKJV

HE IS THE VINE

He was the Son of God, but He wore a crown of thorns. He was the Savior of mankind, yet He was put to death on a roughhewn cross. He offered His healing touch to an unsaved world, and yet the same hands that had healed the sick and raised the dead were pierced with nails.

Jesus Christ, the Son of God, was born into humble circumstances. He walked this earth, not as a ruler of men, but as the Savior of mankind. His crucifixion, a torturous punishment that was intended to end His life and His reign, instead became the pivotal event in the history of all humanity. Christ sacrificed His life on the cross so that we might have eternal life. This gift, freely given by God's only begotten Son, is the priceless possession of everyone who accepts Him as Lord and Savior.

Why did Christ endure the humiliation and torture of the cross? He did it for you. His love is as near as your next breath, as personal as your next thought, more essential than your next heartbeat. And what must you do in response to the Savior's gifts? You must accept His love, praise His name, and share His message of salvation. And, you must conduct yourself in a manner that demonstrates to all the world that your acquaintance with the Master is not a passing fancy but that it is, instead, the cornerstone and the touchstone of your life.

MORE THOUGHTS ABOUT JESUS

Had Jesus been the Word become word, He would have spun theories about life, but since He was the Word become flesh, He put shoes on all His theories and made them walk.

E. Stanley Jones

Tell me the story of Jesus. Write on my heart every word. Tell me the story most precious, sweetest that ever was heard.

Fanny Crosby

Jesus was the perfect reflection of God's nature in every situation He encountered during His time here on earth.

Bill Hybels

The crucial question for each of us is this: What do you think of Jesus, and do you yet have a personal acquaintance with Him?

Hannah Whitall Smith

Christians see sin for what it is: willful rebellion against the rulership of God in their lives. And in turning from their sin, they have embraced God's only means of dealing with sin: Jesus.

Kay Arthur

In your greatest weakness, turn to your greatest strength, Jesus, and hear Him say, "My grace is sufficient for you, for My strength is made perfect in weakness" (2 Corinthians 12:9, NKJV).

Lisa Whelchel

Sold for thirty pieces of silver, He redeemed the world.

R. G. Lee

A WORD TO THE WISE

Jesus is the light of the world. God wants Him to be the light of your life.

Ask, and it will be given to you;
seek, and you will find;
knock, and it will be opened to you.
For everyone who asks receives,
and he who seeks finds,
and to him who knocks it will be opened.

Matthew 7:7-8 NKJV

ASK HIM FOR THE THINGS YOU NEED

How often do you ask God for His help and His wisdom? Occasionally? Intermittently? Whenever you experience a crisis? Hopefully not. Hopefully, you've acquired the habit of asking for God's assistance early and often. And hopefully, you have learned to seek His guidance in every aspect of your life.

In Matthew 7, God promises that He will guide you if you let Him. Your job is to let Him. But sometimes, you will be tempted to do otherwise. Sometimes, you'll be tempted to go along with the crowd; other times, you'll be tempted to do things your way, not God's way. When you feel those temptations, resist them.

God has promised that when you ask for His help, He will not withhold it. So ask. Ask Him to meet the needs of your day. Ask Him to lead you, to protect you, and to correct you. And trust the answers He gives.

God stands at the door and waits. When you knock, He opens. When you ask, He answers. Your task, of course, is to seek His guidance prayerfully, confidently, and often.

MORE THOUGHTS ABOUT ASKING GOD

Some people think God does not like to be troubled with our constant asking. But, the way to trouble God is not to come at all.

D. L. Moody

When will we realize that we're not troubling God with our questions and concerns? His heart is open to hear us— His touch nearer than our next thought—as if no one in the world existed but us. Our very personal God wants to hear from us personally.

Gigi Graham Tchividjian

All we have to do is to acknowledge our need, move from self-sufficiency to dependence, and ask God to become our hiding place.

Bill Hybels

God uses our most stumbling, faltering faith-steps as the open door to His doing for us "more than we ask or think."

Catherine Marshall

Often I have made a request of God with earnest pleadings even backed up with Scripture, only to have Him say "No" because He had something better in store.

Ruth Bell Graham

God makes prayer as easy as possible for us. He's completely approachable and available, and He'll never mock or upbraid us for bringing our needs before Him.

Shirley Dobson

Notice that we must ask. And we will sometimes struggle to hear and struggle with what we hear. But personally, it's worth it. I'm after the path of life—and he alone knows it.

John Eldredge

A WORD TO THE WISE

If you sincerely want to guard your steps, ask for God's help.

VERSE 14

You shall have no other gods before Me.
Exodus 20:3 NKJV

PUTTING GOD FIRST

Is God your top priority? Have you given His Son your heart, your soul, your talents, and your time? Or are you in the habit of giving God little more than a few hours on Sunday morning? The answers to these questions will determine how you prioritize your days and your life.

As you contemplate your own relationship with God, remember this: all of mankind is engaged in the practice of worship. Some people choose to worship God and, as a result, reap the joy that He intends for His children. Others distance themselves from God by worshiping such things as earthly possessions or personal gratification. . . . and when they do so, they suffer.

In the book of Exodus, God warns that we should place no gods before Him. Yet all too often, we place our Lord in second, third, or fourth place as we worship the gods of pride, greed, power, or lust.

When we place our desires for material possessions above our love for God—or when we yield to temptations of the flesh—we find ourselves engaged in a struggle that is similar to the one Jesus faced when He was tempted by Satan. In the wilderness, Satan offered Jesus earthly power and unimaginable riches, but Jesus turned Satan away and chose instead to worship God. We must do likewise by putting God first and worshipping only Him.

Does God rule your heart? Make certain that the honest answer to this question is a resounding yes. In the life of every righteous believer, God comes first. And that's precisely the place that He deserves in your heart, too.

You must never sacrifice your relationship
with God for the sake of a relationship
with another person.

Charles Stanley

MORE THOUGHTS ABOUT PUTTING GOD FIRST

It is impossible to please God doing things motivated by and produced by the flesh.

Bill Bright

A man's spiritual health is exactly proportional to his love for God.

C. S. Lewis

Jesus Christ is the first and last, author and finisher, beginning and end, alpha and omega, and by Him all other things hold together. He must be first or nothing. God never comes next!

Vance Havner

Make God's will the focus of your life day by day. If you seek to please Him and Him alone, you'll find yourself satisfied with life.

Kay Arthur

A WORD TO THE WISE

As you establish priorities for your day and your life, God deserves first place. And you deserve the experience of putting Him there.

VERSE 15

I am come that they might have life,
and that they might have it more abundantly.

John 10:10 KJV

ACCEPTING
GOD'S ABUNDANCE

The 10th chapter of John tells us that Christ came to earth so that our lives might be filled with abundance. But what, exactly, did Jesus mean when He promised "life . . . more abundantly"? Was He referring to material possessions or financial wealth? Hardly. Jesus offers a different kind of abundance: a spiritual richness that extends beyond the temporal boundaries of this world.

Is material abundance part of God's plan for our lives? Perhaps. But in every circumstance of life, during times of wealth or times of want, God will provide us what we need if we trust Him (Matthew 6). May we, as believers, claim the riches of Christ Jesus every day that we live, and may we share His blessings with all who cross our path.

MORE THOUGHTS ABOUT ABUNDANCE

The only way you can experience abundant life is to surrender your plans to Him.

Charles Stanley

God's riches are beyond anything we could ask or even dare to imagine! If my life gets gooey and stale, I have no excuse.

Barbara Johnson

God loves you and wants you to experience peace and life—abundant and eternal.

Billy Graham

Yes, we were created for His holy pleasure, but we will ultimately—if not immediately—find much pleasure in His pleasure.

Beth Moore

It would be wrong to have a "poverty complex," for to think ourselves paupers is to deny either the King's riches or to deny our being His children.

Catherine Marshall

Jesus wants Life for us, Life with a capital L.

John Eldredge

The gift of God is eternal life, spiritual life, abundant life through faith in Jesus Christ, the Living Word of God.

Anne Graham Lotz

The Bible says that being a Christian is not only a great way to die, but it's also the best way to live.

Bill Hybels

People, places, and things were never meant to give us life. God alone is the author of a fulfilling life.

Gary Smalley & John Trent

Jesus intended for us to be overwhelmed by the blessings of regular days. He said it was the reason he had come: "I am come that they might have life, and that they might have it more abundantly."

Gloria Gaither

A WORD TO THE WISE

God wants to shower you with abundance—your job is to let Him.

VERSE 16

Choose for yourselves today the one
you will worship . . . .
As for me and my family,
we will worship the Lord.

Joshua 24:15 Holman CSB

A FAMILY THAT SERVES GOD

In a world filled with countless obligations and frequent frustrations, we may be tempted to take our families for granted. But God intends otherwise.

Our families are precious gifts from our Father in heaven. If we are to be the righteous men and women that God intends, we must care for our loved ones by making time for them, even when the demands of the day are great.

Undeniably, these are difficult days for Christian households; never have distractions and temptations been greater. But, thankfully, God is bigger than all our challenges.

No family is perfect, and neither is yours. But, despite the inevitable challenges, obligations, and hurt feelings of family life, your clan is God's blessing to you. That little band of men, women, kids, and babies is a priceless treasure on temporary loan from the Father above. Give thanks to the Giver for the gift of family . . . and act accordingly.

Living life with a consistent spiritual walk
deeply influences those we love most.

Vonette Bright

MORE THOUGHTS ABOUT FAMILY

More than any other single factor in a person's formative years, family life forges character.

John Maxwell

One way or the other, God, who thought up the family in the first place, has the very best idea of how to bring sense to the chaos of broken relationships we see all around us. I really believe that if I remain still and listen a lot, He will share some solutions with me so I can share them with others.

Jill Briscoe

A family is a place where principles are hammered and honed on the anvil of everyday living.

Charles Swindoll

A home is a place where we find direction.

Gigi Graham Tchividjian

A WORD TO THE WISE

Your family is a precious gift from above, a gift that should be treasured, nurtured, and loved.

VERSE 17

For by grace you are saved through faith,
and this is not from yourselves;
it is God's gift—not from works,
so that no one can boast.

Ephesians 2:8-9 Holman CSB

THE GIFT OF GRACE

In the second chapter of Ephesians, God promises that we will be saved by faith, not by works. It's no wonder, then, that someone once said that GRACE stands for God's Redemption At Christ's Expense. It's true—God sent His Son so that we might be redeemed from our sins. In doing so, our Heavenly Father demonstrated His infinite mercy and His infinite love. We have received countless gifts from God, but none can compare with the gift of salvation. God's grace is the ultimate gift, and we owe Him the ultimate in thanksgiving.

The gift of eternal life is the priceless possession of everyone who accepts God's Son as Lord and Savior. We return our Savior's love by welcoming Him into our hearts and sharing His message and His love. When we do so, we are blessed not today and forever.

How beautiful it is to learn
that grace isn't fragile,
and that in the family of God
we can fail and not be a failure.

—

Gloria Gaither

MORE THOUGHTS ABOUT GRACE

God's grand strategy, birthed in his grace toward us in Christ, and nurtured through the obedience of disciplined faith, is to release us into the redeemed life of our heart, knowing it will lead us back to him even as the North Star guides a ship across the vast unknown surface of the ocean.

John Eldredge

In the depths of our sin, Christ died for us. He did not wait for persons to get as close as possible through obedience to the law and righteous living.

Beth Moore

No one is beyond his grace. No situation, anywhere on earth, it too hard for God.

Jim Cymbala

God shields us from most of the things we fear, but when He chooses not to shield us, He unfailingly allots grace in the measure needed.

Elisabeth Elliot

A WORD TO THE WISE

Remember that His grace is enough . . . God promises that His grace is sufficient for your needs. Believe Him.

VERSE 18

Everyone must be quick to hear,
slow to speak, and slow to anger,
for man's anger does not accomplish
God's righteousness.

James 1:19-20 Holman CSB

THE FUTILITY OF ANGER

If you're like most people, you know a thing or two (or three) about anger. After all, everybody gets mad occasionally, and you're probably no exception.

Anger is a natural human emotion that is sometimes necessary and appropriate. Even Jesus became angry when confronted with the moneychangers in the temple (Matthew 21). Righteous indignation is an appropriate response to evil, but God does not intend that anger should rule our lives. Far from it.

Temper tantrums are usually unproductive, unattractive, unforgettable, and unnecessary. Perhaps that's why Proverbs 16:32 states that, "Controlling your temper is better than capturing a city" (NCV).

If you've allowed anger to become a regular visitor at your house, you should pray for wisdom, for patience, and for a heart that is so filled with forgiveness that it contains no room for bitterness. God will help you terminate your tantrums if you ask Him—and that's a good thing because anger and peace cannot coexist in the same mind.

If you permit yourself to throw too many tantrums, you will forfeit—at least for now—the peace that might otherwise be yours through Christ. So obey God's Word by turning away from anger today and every day. You'll be glad you did, and so will your family and friends.

MORE THOUGHTS ABOUT ANGER

When you strike out in anger, you may miss the other person, but you will always hit yourself.

Jim Gallery

Life is too short to spend it being angry, bored, or dull.

Barbara Johnson

Anger is the noise of the soul; the unseen irritant of the heart; the relentless invader of silence.

Max Lucado

When you get hot under the collar, make sure your heart is prayer-conditioned.

Anonymous

When something robs you of your peace of mind, ask yourself if it is worth the energy you are expending on it. If not, then put it out of your mind in an act of discipline. Every time the thought of "it" returns, refuse it.

Kay Arthur

The hard part about being a praying wife is maintaining a pure heart. If you have resentment, anger, unforgiveness, or an ungodly attitude—even if there's good reason for it—you'll have a difficult time seeing answers to your prayers. But if you can release those feelings to God in total honesty, there is nothing that can change a marriage more dramatically.

Stormie Omartian

Get rid of the poison of built-up anger and the acid of long-term resentment.

Charles Swindoll

A WORD TO THE WISE

Angry words are dangerous to your emotional and spiritual health, not to mention your relationships. So treat anger as an uninvited guest, and usher it away as quickly—and as quietly—as possible.

Therefore,
whatever you want others to do for you,
do also the same for them—
this is the Law and the Prophets.

Matthew 7:12 Holman CSB

THE GOLDEN RULE

The words of Matthew 7:12 remind us that, as believers in Christ, we are commanded to treat others as we wish to be treated. This commandment is, indeed, the Golden Rule for Christians of every generation. When we weave the thread of kindness into the very fabric of our lives, we give glory to the One who gave His life for ours.

Because we are imperfect human beings, we are, on occasion, selfish, thoughtless, or cruel. But God commands us to behave otherwise. He teaches us to rise above our own imperfections and to treat others with unselfishness and love. When we observe God's Golden Rule, we help build His kingdom here on earth. And, when we share the love of Christ, we share a priceless gift; may we share it today and every day that we live.

In your desire to share the gospel,
you may be the only Jesus
someone else will ever meet.
Be real and be involved
with people.

—

Barbara Johnson

MORE THOUGHTS ABOUT THE GOLDEN RULE

It is one of the most beautiful compensations of life that no one can sincerely try to help another without helping herself.

Barbara Johnson

The golden rule to follow to obtain spiritual understanding is not one of intellectual pursuit, but one of obedience.

Oswald Chambers

Choices can change our lives profoundly. The choice to mend a broken relationship, to say "yes" to a difficult assignment, to lay aside some important work to play with a child, to visit some forgotten person—these small choices may affect many lives eternally.

Gloria Gaither

Your light is the truth of the Gospel message itself as well as your witness as to who Jesus is and what He has done for you. Don't hide it.

Anne Graham Lotz

A WORD TO THE WISE

When in doubt, be a little kinder than necessary.

Cast thy burden upon the LORD,
and he shall sustain thee:
he shall never suffer the righteous to be moved.
Psalm 55:22 KJV

WHERE TO PLACE YOUR BURDENS

God's Word contains promises upon which we, as Christians, can and must depend. The Bible is a priceless gift, a tool that God intends for us to use in every aspect of our lives. Too many Christians, however, keep their spiritual tool kits tightly closed and out of sight.

Psalm 55:22 instructs us to cast our burdens upon the Lord. And that's perfect advice for men, women, and children alike.

Are you tired? Discouraged? Fearful? Be comforted and trust the promises that God has made to you. Are you worried or anxious? Be confident in God's power. He will never desert you. Do you see a difficult future ahead? Be courageous and call upon God. He will protect you and then use you according to His purposes. Are you confused?

Listen to the quiet voice of your Heavenly Father. He is not a God of confusion. Talk with Him; listen to Him; trust Him, and trust His promises. He is steadfast, and He is your Protector . . . forever.

MORE THOUGHTS ABOUT GOD'S SUPPORT

He stands fast as your rock, steadfast as your safeguard, sleepless as your watcher, valiant as your champion.

C. H. Spurgeon

Faith is not merely you holding on to God—it is God holding on to you.

E. Stanley Jones

God wants to reveal Himself as your Heavenly Father. When you are hurting, you can run to Him and crawl up into His lap. When you wonder which way to turn, you can grasp His strong hand, and He'll guide you along life's path. When everything around you is falling apart, you'll feel your Father's arm around your shoulder to hold you together.

Lisa Whelchel

Once we recognize our need for Jesus, then the building of our faith begins. It is a daily, moment-by-moment life of absolute dependence upon Him for everything.

Catherine Marshall

The last and greatest lesson that the soul has to learn is the fact that God, and God alone, is enough for all its needs. This is the lesson that all His dealings with us are meant to teach; and this is the crowning discovery of our whole Christian life. God is enough!

Hannah Whitall Smith

God uses our most stumbling, faltering faith-steps as the open door to His doing for us "more than we ask or think."

Catherine Marshall

Measure the size of the obstacles against the size of God.

Beth Moore

A WORD TO THE WISE

God can handle it. Corrie ten Boom advised, "God's all-sufficiency is a major. Your inability is a minor. Major in majors, not in minors." Enough said.

You will show me the path of life;
in Your presence is fullness of joy;
at Your right hand are pleasures forevermore.

Psalm 16:11 NKJV

HE WILL SHOW YOU
THE PATH

Life is best lived on purpose. And purpose, like everything else in the universe, begins in the heart of God. Whether you realize it or not, God has a direction for your life, a divine calling, a path along which He intends to lead you. When you welcome God into your heart and establish a genuine relationship with Him, He will begin—and He will continue—to make His purposes known.

Each morning, as the sun rises in the east, you welcome a new day, one that is filled to the brim with opportunities, with possibilities, and with God. As you contemplate God's blessings in your own life, you should prayerfully seek His guidance for the day ahead.

Discovering God's unfolding purpose for your life is a daily journey, a journey guided by the teachings of God's

Holy Word. As you reflect upon God's promises and upon the meaning that those promises hold for you, ask God to lead you throughout the coming day. Let your Heavenly Father direct your steps; concentrate on what God wants you to do now, and leave the distant future in hands that are far more capable than your own: His hands.

Sometimes, God's intentions will be clear to you; other times, God's plan will seem uncertain at best. But even on those difficult days when you are unsure which way to turn, you must never lose sight of these overriding facts: God created you for a reason; He has important work for you to do; and He's waiting patiently for you to do it. So why not begin today?

MORE THOUGHTS ABOUT LIVING ON PURPOSE

How much of our lives are, well, so daily. How often our hours are filled with the mundane, seemingly unimportant things that have to be done, whether at home or work. These very "daily" tasks could become a celebration of praise. "It is through consecration," someone has said, "that drudgery is made divine."

Gigi Graham Tchividjian

Continually restate to yourself what the purpose of your life is.

Oswald Chambers

Only God's chosen task for you will ultimately satisfy. Do not wait until it is too late to realize the privilege of serving Him in His chosen position for you.

Beth Moore

When God speaks to you through the Bible, prayer, circumstances, the church, or in some other way, he has a purpose in mind for your life.

Henry Blackaby and Claude King

Yesterday is just experience but tomorrow is glistening with purpose—and today is the channel leading from one to the other.

Barbara Johnson

In the very place where God has put us, whatever its limitations, whatever kind of work it may be, we may indeed serve the Lord Christ.

Elisabeth Elliot

A WORD TO THE WISE

God has a plan for your life, a definite purpose that you can fulfill . . . or not. Your challenge is to pray for God's guidance and to follow wherever He leads.

VERSE 22

*Now by this we know that we know Him,
if we keep His commandments.*

1 John 2:3 NKJV

OBEDIENCE NOW

Obedience to God is determined not by words, but by deeds. Talking about righteousness is easy; living righteously is far more difficult, especially in today's temptation-filled world.

Since God created Adam and Eve, we human beings have been rebelling against our Creator. Why? Because we are unwilling to trust God's Word, and we are unwilling to follow His commandments. God has given us a guidebook for righteous living called the Holy Bible. It contains thorough instructions which, if followed, lead to fulfillment, abundance, and salvation. But, if we choose to ignore God's commandments, the results are as predictable as they are tragic.

When we seek righteousness in our own lives—and when we seek the companionship of those who do likewise—we reap the spiritual rewards that God intends for our lives. When we behave ourselves as godly men and women, we honor God. When we live righteously and according to God's commandments, He blesses us in ways that we cannot fully understand.

Do you seek God's peace and His blessings? Then obey Him. When you're faced with a difficult choice or a powerful temptation, seek God's counsel and trust the counsel He gives. Invite God into your heart and live according to His commandments. When you do, you will be blessed today, tomorrow, and forever.

Obedience is the outward expression
of your love of God.

Henry Blackaby

MORE THOUGHTS ABOUT OBEDIENCE

Believe and do what God says. The life-changing consequences will be limitless, and the results will be confidence and peace of mind.

Franklin Graham

I don't always like His decisions, but when I choose to obey Him, the act of obedience still "counts" with Him even if I'm not thrilled about it.

Beth Moore

Jesus is Victor. Calvary is the place of victory. Obedience is the pathway of victory. Bible study and prayer is the preparation for victory.

Corrie ten Boom

You may not always see immediate results, but all God wants is your obedience and faithfulness.

Vonette Bright

A WORD TO THE WISE

Because God is just, He rewards good behavior just as surely as He punishes sin. Obedience earns God's pleasure; disobedience doesn't.

VERSE 23

*All Scripture is given by inspiration of God,
and is profitable for doctrine, for reproof,
for correction, for instruction in righteousness,
that the man of God may be complete,
thoroughly equipped for every good work.*
2 Timothy 3:16-17 NKJV

THE USE OF SCRIPTURE

I s Bible study a high priority for you? The answer to this simple question will determine, to a surprising extent, the quality of your life and the direction of your faith.

As you establish priorities for life, you must decide whether God's Word will be a bright spotlight that guides your path every day or a tiny nightlight that occasionally flickers in the dark. The decision to study the Bible—or not—is yours and yours alone. But make no mistake: how you choose to use your Bible will have a profound impact on you and your loved ones.

George Mueller observed, "The vigor of our spiritual lives will be in exact proportion to the place held by the Bible in our lives and in our thoughts." Think of it like this: the more you use your Bible, the more God will use you.

Perhaps you're one of those Christians who owns a bookshelf full of unread Bibles. If so, remember the old saying, "A Bible in the hand is worth two in the bookcase." Or perhaps you're one of those folks who is simply "too busy" to find time for a daily dose of prayer and Bible study. If so, remember the old adage, "It's hard to stumble when you're on your knees."

God's Word can be a roadmap to a place of righteousness and abundance. Make it your roadmap. God's wisdom can be a light to guide your steps. Claim it as your light today, tomorrow, and every day of your life—and then walk confidently in the footsteps of God's only begotten Son.

MORE THOUGHTS ABOUT GOD'S WORD

My meditation and study have shown me that, like God, His Word is holy, everlasting, absolutely true, powerful, personally fair, and never changing.

Bill Bright

The Bible is God's Word to man.

Kay Arthur

Help me, Lord, to be a student of Your Word, that I might be a better servant in Your world.

Jim Gallery

Either God's Word keeps you from sin, or sin keeps you from God's Word.

Corrie ten Boom

God's Word is a light not only to our path but also to our thinking. Place it in your heart today, and you will never walk in darkness.

Joni Eareckson Tada

Walking in faith brings you to the Word of God. There you will be healed, cleansed, fed, nurtured, equipped, and matured.

Kay Arthur

God's voice isn't all that difficult to hear. He sometimes shouts through our pain, whispers to us while we're relaxing on vacation, occasionally, He sings to us in a song, and warns us through the sixty-six books of His written Word. It's right there, ink on paper. Count on it—that book will never lead you astray.

Charles Swindoll

A WORD TO THE WISE

God intends for you to use His Word as your guidebook for life . . . your intentions should be the same.

VERSE 24

To everything there is a season,
a time for every purpose under heaven.

Ecclesiastes 3:1 NKJV

TRUST GOD'S TIMING

Sometimes, the hardest thing to do is to wait. This is especially true when we're in a hurry and when we want things to happen now, if not sooner! But God's plan does not always happen in the way that we would like or at the time of our own choosing. Our task—as thoughtful men and women who trust in a benevolent, all-knowing Father—is to wait patiently for God to reveal Himself.

We humans know precisely what we want, and we know exactly when we want it. But, God has a far better plan for each of us. He has created a world that unfolds according to His own timetable, not ours . . . thank goodness! And if we're wise, we trust Him and we wait patiently for Him. After all, He is trustworthy, and He always knows best.

Your times are in His hands.
He's in charge of the timetable,
so wait patiently.

—

Kay Arthur

More Thoughts About God's Timing

Grass that is here today and gone tomorrow does not require much time to mature. A big oak tree that lasts for generations requires much more time to grow and mature. God is concerned about your life through eternity. Allow Him to take all the time He needs to shape you for His purposes. Larger assignments will require longer periods of preparation.

Henry Blackaby

God does not promise to keep us out of the storms and floods, but He does promise to sustain us in the storm, and then bring us out in due time for His glory when the storm has done its work.

Warren Wiersbe

God's delays and His ways can be confusing because the process God uses to accomplish His will can go against human logic and common sense.

Anne Graham Lotz

A Word to the Wise

You don't know precisely what you need—or when you need it—but God does. So trust His timing.

Guard your heart above all else,
for it is the source of life.

Proverbs 4:23 Holman CSB

GUARD YOUR HEART

You are near and dear to God. He loves you more than you can imagine, and He wants the very best for you. And one more thing: God wants you to guard your heart.

Every day, you are faced with choices . . . more choices than you can count. You can do the right thing, or not. You can be prudent, or not. You can be kind, generous, and obedient to God. Or not.

Today, the world will offer you countless opportunities to let down your guard and, by doing so, make needless mistakes that may injure you or your loved ones. So be watchful and obedient. Guard your heart by giving it to your Heavenly Father; it is safe with Him.

Our actions are seen by people,
but our motives
are monitored by God.

—

Franklin Graham

MORE THOUGHTS ABOUT
GUARDING YOUR HEART

To lose heart is to lose everything.

John Eldredge

The God who dwells in heaven is willing to dwell also in the heart of the humble believer.

Warren Wiersbe

The more wisdom enters our hearts, the more we will be able to trust our hearts in difficult situations.

John Eldredge

We can't stop the Adversary from whispering in our ears, but we can refuse to listen, and we can definitely refuse to respond.

Liz Curtis Higgs

A WORD TO THE WISE

Today, think about the value of living a life that is pleasing to God. And while you're at it, think about the rewards that are likely to be yours when you do the right thing day in and day out.

VERSE 26

*Then He said to them all, "If anyone desires
to come after Me, let him deny himself,
and take up his cross daily, and follow Me.
For whoever desires to save his life will lose it,
but whoever loses his life for My sake will save it."*

Luke 9:23-24 NKJV

FOLLOW HIM

Jesus walks with you. Are you walking with Him?
Hopefully, you will choose to walk with Him today
and every day of your life.

Jesus loved you so much that He endured unspeakable
humiliation and suffering for you. How will you respond to
Christ's sacrifice? Will you follow the instructions of Luke
9:23 by taking up His cross and following Him? Or will you
choose another path? When you place your hopes squarely
at the foot of the cross, when you place Jesus squarely at
the center of your life, you will be blessed. If you seek to be
a worthy disciple of Jesus, you must acknowledge that He
never comes "next." He is always first.

Do you hope to fulfill God's purpose for your life? Do
you seek a life of abundance and peace? Do you intend to

be Christian, not just in name, but in deed? Then follow Christ. Follow Him by picking up His cross today and every day that you live. When you do, you will quickly discover that Christ's love has the power to change everything, including you.

MORE THOUGHTS ABOUT FOLLOWING JESUS

As we live moment by moment under the control of the Spirit, His character, which is the character of Jesus, becomes evident to those around us.

Anne Graham Lotz

Peter said, "No, Lord!" But he had to learn that one cannot say "No" while saying "Lord" and that one cannot say "Lord" while saying "No."

Corrie ten Boom

We have in Jesus Christ a perfect example of how to put God's truth into practice.

Bill Bright

Think of this—we may live together with Him here and now, a daily walking with Him who loved us and gave Himself for us.

Elisabeth Elliot

Will you, with a glad and eager surrender, hand yourself and all that concerns you over into his hands? If you will do this, your soul will begin to know something of the joy of union with Christ.

Hannah Whitall Smith

A disciple is a follower of Christ. That means you take on His priorities as your own. His agenda becomes your agenda. His mission becomes your mission.

Charles Stanley

The Christian faith is meant to be lived moment by moment. It isn't some broad, general outline—it's a long walk with a real Person. Details count: passing thoughts, small sacrifices, a few encouraging words, little acts of kindness, brief victories over nagging sins.

Joni Eareckson Tada

A WORD TO THE WISE

It takes a radical commitment—and significant sacrifices—to really follow Jesus. And it's worth it.

VERSE 27

As the Father loved Me,
I also have loved you; abide in My love.

John 15:9 NKJV

CHRIST'S LOVE

How much does Christ love us? More than we, as mere mortals, can comprehend. His love is perfect and steadfast. Even though we are fallible and wayward, the Good Shepherd cares for us still. Even though we have fallen far short of the Father's commandments, Christ loves us with a power and depth that are beyond our understanding. The sacrifice that Jesus made upon the cross was made for each of us, and His love endures to the edge of eternity and beyond.

Hannah Whitall Smith spoke to believers of every generation when she advised, "Keep your face upturned to Christ as the flowers do to the sun. Look, and your soul shall live and grow." How true. When we turn our hearts to Jesus, we receive His blessings, His peace, and His grace.

Christ is the ultimate Savior of mankind and the personal Savior of those who believe in Him. As His servants, we should place Him at the very center of our lives. And, every day that God gives us breath, we should share Christ's love and His message with a world that needs both.

Christ's love changes everything. When you accept His gift of grace, you are transformed, not only for today, but also for all eternity. If you haven't already done so, accept Jesus Christ as your personal Savior. He's waiting patiently for you to invite Him into your heart. Please don't make Him wait a single minute longer.

MORE THOUGHTS ABOUT CHRIST'S LOVE

To God be the glory, great things He has done; / So loved He the world that He gave us His Son.

Fanny Crosby

Live your lives in love, the same sort of love which Christ gives us, and which He perfectly expressed when He gave Himself as a sacrifice to God.

Corrie ten Boom

No man ever loved like Jesus. He taught the blind to see and the dumb to speak. He died on the cross to save us. He bore our sins. And now God says, "Because He did, I can forgive you."

Billy Graham

This hard place in which you perhaps find yourself is the very place in which God is giving you opportunity to look only to Him, to spend time in prayer, and to learn long-suffering, gentleness, meekness—in short, to learn the depths of the love that Christ Himself has poured out on all of us.

Elisabeth Elliot

Jesus loves me! This I know, for the Bible tells me so. Little ones to him belong; they are weak, but he is strong. / Yes, Jesus loves me! Yes, Jesus loves me! Yes, Jesus loves me! The Bible tells me so.

Anna B. Warner and Susan Warner

Sometimes Agape really hurts. It broke the heart of God to demonstrate His love to us through Christ but it's ultimate end was salvation.

Beth Moore

A WORD TO THE WISE

Jesus loves you. His love can—and should—be the cornerstone and the touchstone of your life.

VERSE 28

The greatest among you must be a servant.
But those who exalt themselves will be humbled,
and those who humble themselves will be exalted.
Matthew 23:11-12 NKJV

STAYING HUMBLE

As fallible human beings, we have so much to be humble about. Why, then, is humility such a difficult trait for us to master? Precisely because we are fallible human beings. Yet if we are to grow and mature as Christians, we must strive to give credit where credit is due, starting, of course, with God and His only begotten Son.

As Christians, we have been refashioned and saved by Jesus Christ, and that salvation came not because of our own good works but because of God's grace. Thus, we are not "self-made"; we are "God-made," and we are "Christ-saved." How, then, can we be boastful? The answer, of course, is that, if we are honest with ourselves and with our God, we simply can't be boastful . . . we must, instead, be eternally grateful and exceedingly humble. Humility, however, is not easy for most of us. All too often, we are tempted to stick out our chests and say, "Look at me; look what I did!" But, in the quiet moments when we search the depths of our own hearts, we know better. Whatever "it" is, God did that. And He deserves the credit.

MORE THOUGHTS ABOUT HUMILITY

If you know who you are in Christ, your personal ego is not an issue.

Beth Moore

We are never stronger than the moment we admit we are weak.

Beth Moore

That some of my hymns have been dictated by the blessed Holy Spirit I have no doubt; and that others have been the result of deep meditation I know to be true; but that the poet has any right to claim special merit for himself is certainly presumptuous.

Fanny Crosby

All kindness and good deeds, we must keep silent. The result will be an inner reservoir of personality power.

Catherine Marshall

That's what I love about serving God. In His eyes, there are no little people . . . because there are no big people. We are all on the same playing field. We all start at square one. No one has it better than the other, or possesses unfair advantage.

Joni Eareckson Tada

Humility is the fairest and rarest flower that blooms.

Charles Swindoll

I can usually sense that a leading is from the Holy Spirit when it calls me to humble myself, to serve somebody, to encourage somebody, or to give something away. Very rarely will the evil one lead us to do those kind of things.

Bill Hybels

Jesus had a humble heart. If He abides in us, pride will never dominate our lives.

Billy Graham

A WORD TO THE WISE

You must remain humble or face the consequences. Pride does go before the fall, but humility often prevents the fall.

These things have I spoken unto you,
that my joy might remain in you,
and that your joy might be full.

John 15:11 KJV

MAKING HIS JOY YOUR JOY

Christ made it clear: He intends that His joy should become our joy. Yet sometimes, amid the inevitable hustle and bustle of life here on earth, we can forfeit—albeit temporarily—the joy of Christ as we wrestle with the challenges of daily living.

Jonathan Edwards, the 18th-century American clergyman, observed, "Christ is not only a remedy for your weariness and trouble, but He will give you an abundance of the contrary: joy and delight. They who come to Christ do not only come to a resting-place after they have been wandering in a wilderness, but they come to a banqueting-house where they may rest, and where they may feast. They may cease from their former troubles and toils, and they may enter upon a course of delights and spiritual joys."

If, today, your heart is heavy, open the door of your soul to Christ. He will give you peace and joy. And, if you already have the joy of Christ in your heart, share it freely, just as Christ freely shared His joy with you.

MORE THOUGHTS ABOUT JOY

The Christian lifestyle is not one of legalistic do's and don'ts, but one that is positive, attractive, and joyful.

Vonette Bright

Joy is the direct result of having God's perspective on our daily lives and the effect of loving our Lord enough to obey His commands and trust His promises.

Bill Bright

Our sense of joy, satisfaction, and fulfillment in life increases, no matter what the circumstances, if we are in the center of God's will.

Billy Graham

A life of intimacy with God is characterized by joy.

Oswald Chambers

Joy is the heart's harmonious response to the Lord's song of love.

A. W. Tozer

Rejoice, the Lord is King; Your Lord and King adore!
Rejoice, give thanks and sing and triumph evermore.

Charles Wesley

Lord, I thank you for the promise of heaven and the
unexpected moments when you touch my heartstrings
with that longing for my eternal home.

Joni Eareckson Tada

God knows everything. He can manage everything, and
He loves us. Surely this is enough for a fullness of joy that
is beyond words.

Hannah Whitall Smith

God gives to us a heavenly gift called joy, radically different
in quality from any natural joy.

Elisabeth Elliot

A WORD TO THE WISE

Every day, God gives you many reasons to rejoice. The rest
is up to you.

VERSE 30

Rejoice in the Lord always.
Again I will say, rejoice!
Philippians 4:4 NKJV

REJOICE!

Are you living a life of agitation, consternation, or celebration? If you're a believer, it should most certainly be the latter. With Christ as your Savior, every day should be a time of celebration.

Oswald Chambers correctly observed, "Joy is the great note all throughout the Bible." C. S. Lewis echoed that thought when he wrote, "Joy is the serious business of heaven." But, even the most dedicated Christians can, on occasion, forget to celebrate each day for what it is: a priceless gift from God.

Today, celebrate the life that God has given you. Today, put a smile on your face, kind words on your lips, and a song in your heart. Be generous with your praise and free with your encouragement. And then, when you have celebrated life to the full, invite your friends to do likewise. After all, this is God's day, and He has given us clear instructions for its use. We are commanded to rejoice and be glad. So, with no further ado, let the celebration begin . . .

97

If you can forgive the person you were, accept the person you are, and believe in the person you will become, you are headed for joy. So celebrate your life.

—

Barbara Johnson

MORE THOUGHTS ABOUT CELEBRATION

Joy is the direct result of having God's perspective on our daily lives and the effect of loving our Lord enough to obey His commands and trust His promises.

Bill Bright

Christ is the secret, the source, the substance, the center, and the circumference of all true and lasting gladness.

Mrs. Charles E. Cowman

When the dream of our heart is one that God has planted there, a strange happiness flows into us. At that moment, all of the spiritual resources of the universe are released to help us. Our praying is then at one with the will of God and becomes a channel for the Creator's purposes for us and our world.

Catherine Marshall

A WORD TO THE WISE

Every day should be a cause for celebration. By celebrating the gift of life, you protect your heart from the dangers of pessimism, regret, hopelessness, and bitterness.

Do not judge, and you will not be judged.
Do not condemn, and you will not be condemned.
Forgive, and you will be forgiven.

Luke 6:37 Holman CSB

FORGIVENESS: YES, JUDGING: NO

Even the most devoted Christians may fall prey to a powerful yet subtle temptation: the temptation to judge others. But as Christians, we are commanded to refrain from such behavior. The warning of Luke 6:37 is clear: "Do not judge." Yet, as fallible, imperfect human beings living in a stressful world, we are sorely tempted to do otherwise.

As Jesus came upon a young woman who had been condemned by the Pharisees, He spoke not only to the crowd that was gathered there, but also to all generations when He warned, "He that is without sin among you, let him first cast a stone at her" (John 8:7 KJV). Christ's message is clear, and it applies not only to the Pharisees of ancient times, but also to us.

We have all fallen short of God's commandments, and none of us, therefore, are qualified to "cast the first stone."

Thankfully, God has forgiven us, and we, too, must forgive others. As Christian believers, we are warned that to judge others is to invite fearful consequences: to the extent we judge others, so, too, will we be judged by God. Let us refrain, then, from judging our neighbors. Instead, let us forgive them and love them in the same way that God has forgiven us.

Being critical of others, including God,
is one way we try to avoid facing
and judging our own sins.

Warren Wiersbe

MORE THOUGHTS ABOUT JUDGING OTHERS

Judging draws the judgment of others.

Catherine Marshall

Christians think they are prosecuting attorneys or judges, when, in reality, God has called all of us to be witnesses.

Warren Wiersbe

Don't judge other people more harshly than you want God to judge you.

Marie T. Freeman

An individual Christian may see fit to give up all sorts of things for special reasons—marriage, or meat, or beer, or cinema; but the moment he starts saying these things are bad in themselves, or looking down his nose at other people who do use them, he has taken the wrong turn.

C. S. Lewis

A WORD TO THE WISE

To the extent you judge others, so, too, will you be judged. So you must, to the best of your ability, refrain from judgmental thoughts and words.

VERSE 32

Assuredly, I say to you,
inasmuch as you did it to one of the least of these
My brethren, you did it to Me.

Matthew 25:40 NKJV

GENEROSITY NOW

In the busyness and confusion of daily life, it is easy to lose focus, and it is easy to become frustrated. We are imperfect human beings struggling to manage our lives as best we can, but we often fall short. When we are distracted or disappointed, we may neglect to share a kind word or a kind deed. This oversight hurts others, but it hurts us most of all.

Matthew 25:40 warns, "Inasmuch as you did it to one of the least of these My brethren, you did it to Me." When we extend the hand of friendship to those who need it most, God promises His blessings. When we ignore the needs of others—or mistreat them—we risk God's retribution.

Today, slow yourself down and be alert for those who need your smile, your kind words, or your helping hand. Make kindness a centerpiece of your dealings with others. They will be blessed, and you will be, too. When you spread a heaping helping of encouragement and hope to the world, you can't help getting a little bit on yourself.

MORE THOUGHTS ABOUT KINDNESS

When we do little acts of kindness that make life more bearable for someone else, we are walking in love as the Bible commands us.

Barbara Johnson

When you extend hospitality to others, you're not trying to impress people, you're trying to reflect God to them.

Max Lucado

If I am inconsiderate about the comfort of others, or their feelings, or even their little weaknesses; if I am careless about their little hurts and miss opportunities to smooth their way; if I make the sweet running of household wheels more difficult to accomplish, then I know nothing of Calvary's love.

Amy Carmichael

It is one of the most beautiful compensations of life that no one can sincerely try to help another without helping herself.

Barbara Johnson

A little kindly advice is better than a great deal of scolding.

Fanny Crosby

Do all the good you can. By all the means you can. In all the ways you can. In all the places you can. At all the times you can. To all the people you can. As long as you can.

John Wesley

The mark of a Christian is that he will walk the second mile and turn the other cheek. A wise man or woman gives the extra effort, all for the glory of the Lord Jesus Christ.

John Maxwell

Be so preoccupied with good will that you haven't room for ill will.

E. Stanley Jones

When we Christians are too busy to care for each other, we're simply too busy for our own good . . . and for God's.

Marie T. Freeman

A WORD TO THE WISE

Kind words have echoes that last a lifetime and beyond.

*Finally, brethren, whatever things are true,
whatever things are noble,
whatever things are just, whatever things are pure,
whatever things are lovely, whatever things are of
good report, if there is any virtue and if there is
anything praiseworthy—meditate on these things.*

Philippians 4:8 NKJV

THE DIRECTION OF YOUR THOUGHTS

How will you direct your thoughts today? Will you obey the words of Philippians 4:8 by dwelling upon those things that are true, noble, and just? Or will you allow your thoughts to be hijacked by the negativity that seems to dominate our troubled world?

Are you fearful, angry, bored, or worried? Are you so preoccupied with the concerns of this day that you fail to thank God for the promise of eternity? Are you confused, bitter, or pessimistic? If so, God wants to have a little talk with you.

God intends that you be an ambassador for Him, an enthusiastic, hope-filled Christian. But God won't force you to adopt a positive attitude. It's up to you to think positively about your blessings and opportunities . . . or not. So, today and every day hereafter, celebrate this life that God has given you by focusing your thoughts and your energies upon "things that are excellent and worthy of praise." Today, count your blessings instead of your hardships. And thank the Giver of all things good for gifts that are simply too numerous to count.

Attitude is the mind's paintbrush;
it can color any situation.

Barbara Johnson

More Thoughts About Your Thoughts

Whether we think of, or speak to, God, whether we act or suffer for him, all is prayer when we have no other object than his love and the desire of pleasing him.

John Wesley

It is the thoughts and intents of the heart that shape a person's life.

John Eldredge

No more imperfect thoughts. No more sad memories. No more ignorance. My redeemed body will have a redeemed mind. Grant me a foretaste of that perfect mind as you mirror your thoughts in me today.

Joni Eareckson Tada

The things we think are the things that feed our souls. If we think on pure and lovely things, we shall grow pure and lovely like them; and the converse is equally true.

Hannah Whitall Smith

A Word to the Wise

Either you can control your thoughts, or they most certainly will control you.

I have come as a light into the world,
that whoever believes in Me
should not abide in darkness.

John 12:46 NKJV

JESUS IS THE LIGHT

The words of John 12:46 teach us that Jesus is the light of the world. And, John 14:6-7 instructs us that Jesus is, "the way, the truth, and the life." Without Christ, we are as far removed from salvation as the east is removed from the west. And without Christ, we can never know the ultimate truth: God's truth.

Truth is God's way: He commands His believers to live in truth, and He rewards those who do so. Jesus is the personification of God's liberating truth, a truth that offers salvation to mankind.

Do you seek to walk with God? Do you seek to feel His presence and His peace? Then you must walk in truth; you must walk in the light; you must walk with the Savior. There is simply no other way.

When we are in a situation where
Jesus is all we have,
we soon discover
He is all we really need.

—

Gigi Graham Tchividjian

MORE THOUGHTS ABOUT JESUS

The key to my understanding of the Bible is a personal relationship to Jesus Christ.

Oswald Chambers

There was One, who for "us sinners and our salvation," left the glories of heaven and sojourned upon this earth in weariness and woe, amid those who hated Him and finally took His life.

Lottie Moon

When you can't see him, trust him. Jesus is closer than you ever dreamed.

Max Lucado

In your greatest weakness, turn to your greatest strength, Jesus, and hear Him say, "My grace is sufficient for you, for My strength is made perfect in weakness" (2 Corinthians 12:9, NKJV).

Lisa Whelchel

A WORD TO THE WISE

You are a light upon the world around you. Make sure that your light is both bright and good.

111

VERSE 35

Unless the Lord builds a house,
its builders labor over it in vain;
unless the Lord watches over a city,
the watchman stays alert in vain.

Psalm 127:1 Holman CSB

HE WATCHES OVER US

Have you ever faced challenges that seemed too big to handle? Have you ever faced big problems that, despite your best efforts, simply could not be solved? If so, you know how uncomfortable it is to feel helpless in the face of difficult circumstances. Thankfully, even when there's nowhere else to turn, you can turn your thoughts and prayers to God, and He will respond.

God's hand uplifts those who turn their hearts and prayers to Him. Count yourself among that number. When you do, you can live courageously and joyfully, knowing that "this too will pass"—but that God's love for you will not. And you can draw strength from the knowledge that you are a marvelous creation, loved, protected, and uplifted by the ever-present hand of God.

More Thoughts About God's Protection

There is no safer place to live than the center of His will.

Calvin Miller

The task ahead of us is never as great as the Power behind us.

Anonymous

When you fall and skin your knees and skin your heart, He'll pick you up.

Charles Stanley

Trials are not enemies of faith but opportunities to reveal God's faithfulness.

Barbara Johnson

Gather the riches of God's promises which can strengthen you in the time when there will be no freedom.

Corrie ten Boom

Our future may look fearfully intimidating, yet we can look up to the Engineer of the Universe, confident that nothing escapes His attention or slips out of the control of those strong hands.

Elisabeth Elliot

In all the old castles of England, there was a place called the keep. It was always the strongest and best protected place in the castle, and in it were hidden all who were weak and helpless and unable to defend themselves in times of danger. Shall we be afraid to hide ourselves in the keeping power of our Divine Keeper, who neither slumbers nor sleeps, and who has promised to preserve our going out and our coming in, from this time forth and even forever more?

Hannah Whitall Smith

My case is urgent, and I do not see how I am to be delivered; but this is no business of mine. He who makes the promise will find ways and means of keeping it. It is mine to obey His command; it is not mine to direct His counsels. I am His servant, not His solicitor. I call upon Him, and He will deliver.

C. H. Spurgeon

A WORD TO THE WISE

When you are in the center of God's will, you are in the center of God's protection.

VERSE 36

Blessed are the merciful,
because they will be shown mercy.
Matthew 5:7 Holman CSB

BE MERCIFUL

If we wish to build lasting relationships, we must learn how to forgive. Why? Because our loved ones are imperfect (as are we). How often must we forgive our spouses and our friends? More times than we can count; to do otherwise is to disobey God.

Are you easily frustrated by the inevitable imperfections of others? Are you easily angered? Do you sometimes hold on to feelings of bitterness and regret. If so, perhaps you need a refresher course in the art of forgiveness.

Perhaps granting forgiveness is hard for you. If so, you are not alone. Genuine, lasting forgiveness is often difficult to achieve—difficult but not impossible. Thankfully, with God's help, all things are possible, and that includes forgiveness. But even though God is willing to help, He expects you to do some of the work.

If there exists even one person, alive or dead, whom you have not forgiven (and that includes yourself), follow

God's commandment and His will for your life: forgive. Bitterness, anger, and regret are not part of God's plan for your life. Forgiveness is.

Forgiveness is the precondition of love.

Catherine Marshall

MORE THOUGHTS ABOUT LOVE AND FORGIVENESS

Revenge is the raging fire that consumes the arsonist.

Max Lucado

When God forgives, He forgets. He buries our sins in the sea and puts a sign on the shore saying, "No Fishing Allowed."

Corrie ten Boom

Jesus had a forgiving and understanding heart. If he lives within us, mercy will temper our relationships with our fellow men.

Billy Graham

God expects us to forgive others as He has forgiven us; we are to follow His example by having a forgiving heart.

Vonette Bright

The more you practice the art of forgiving, the quicker you'll master the art of living.

Marie T. Freeman

A WORD TO THE WISE

How hard is it to love your enemies? You'll never know until you try . . . so try!

VERSE 37

Make no friendship with an angry man,
and with a furious man do not go,
lest you learn his ways and set a snare for your soul.

Proverbs 22:24-25 NKJV

DEALING WITH
DIFFICULT PEOPLE

Face it: sometimes people can be difficult to deal with . . . very, very difficult. When other people are unkind to you, you may be tempted to strike back, either verbally or in some other way. Resist that temptation. Instead, remember that God corrects other people's behaviors in His own way, and He doesn't need your help (even if you're totally convinced that He does).

So when other people behave cruelly, foolishly, or impulsively—as they will from time to time—don't respond in kind. Instead, speak up for yourself as politely as you can, and walk away. Then, forgive everybody as quickly as you can and leave the rest up to God.

MORE THOUGHTS ABOUT DIFFICULT PEOPLE

Sour godliness is the devil's religion.

John Wesley

You can be sure you are abiding in Christ if you are able to have a Christlike love toward the people that irritate you the most.

Vonette Bright

A keen sense of humor helps us to overlook the unbecoming, understand the unconventional, tolerate the unpleasant, overcome the unexpected, and outlast the unbearable.

Billy Graham

A pessimist is someone who believes that when her cup runneth over she'll need a mop.

Barbara Johnson

We are all fallen creatures and all very hard to live with.

C. S. Lewis

If some hypocrites do intrude among us, it should not astonish us.

C. H. Spurgeon

Discouraged people, if they must be discouraged, ought, at least, to keep their discouragements to themselves, hidden away in the privacy of their own bosoms lest they should discourage the hearts of their brethren.

Hannah Whitall Smith

When something robs you of your peace of mind, ask yourself if it is worth the energy you are expending on it. If not, then put it out of your mind in an act of discipline. Every time the thought of "it" returns, refuse it.

Kay Arthur

A WORD TO THE WISE

If you can't find it in your heart to forgive those who have hurt you, you're hurting yourself more than you're hurting anyone else. But remember: forgiveness should not be confused with enabling. Even after you've forgiven the difficult person in your life, you are not compelled to accept continued mistreatment from him or her.

VERSE 38

But Jesus looked at them and said to them,
"With men this is impossible,
but with God all things are possible."
Matthew 19:26 NKJV

WITH GOD,
ALL THINGS ARE POSSIBLE

Sometimes, because we are imperfect human beings with limited understanding and limited faith, we place limitations on God. But, God's power has no limitations. God will work miracles in our lives if we trust Him with everything we have and everything we are. When we do, we experience the miraculous results of His endless love and His awesome power.

Miracles, both great and small, are an integral part of everyday life, but usually, we are too busy or too cynical to notice God's handiwork. We don't expect to see miracles, so we simply overlook them.

Do you lack the faith that God can work miracles in your own life? If so, it's time to reconsider. If you have allowed yourself to become a "doubting Thomas," you are attempting to place limitations on a God who has none. Instead of doubting your Heavenly Father, you must trust Him. Then, you must wait and watch . . . because something miraculous is going to happen to you, and it might just happen today.

Only God can move mountains,
but faith and prayer can move God.

E. M. Bounds

More Thoughts About Miracles

There is Someone who makes possible what seems completely impossible.

Catherine Marshall

I could go through this day oblivious to the miracles all around me or I could tune in and "enjoy."

Gloria Gaither

Here lies the tremendous mystery—that God should be all-powerful, yet refuse to coerce. He summons us to cooperation. We are honored in being given the opportunity to participate in His good deeds. Remember how He asked for help in performing His miracles: Fill the water pots, stretch out your hand, distribute the loaves.

Elisabeth Elliot

Are you looking for a miracle? If you keep your eyes wide open and trust in God, you won't have to look very far.

Marie T. Freeman

A Word to the Wise

God is in the business of doing miraculous things. You should never be afraid to ask Him for a miracle.

Make a joyful noise unto the LORD,
all ye lands.
Serve the LORD with gladness:
come before his presence with singing.

Psalm 100:1-2 KJV

MAKE A JOYFUL NOISE

When is the best time to "make a joyful noise" by praising God? In church? Before dinner is served? When we tuck little children into bed? None of the above. The best time to praise God is all day, every day, to the greatest extent we can, with thanksgiving in our hearts, and with a song on our lips.

Too many of us, even well-intentioned believers, tend to compartmentalize our waking hours into a few familiar categories: work, rest, play, family time, and worship. To do so is a mistake. Worship and praise should be woven into the fabric of everything we do; it should never be relegated to a weekly three-hour visit to church on Sunday morning.

Theologian Wayne Oates once admitted, "Many of my prayers are made with my eyes open. You see, it seems I'm always praying about something, and it's not always convenient—or safe—to close my eyes." Dr. Oates understood that God always hears our prayers and that the relative position of our eyelids is of no concern to Him.

Today, find a little more time to lift your concerns to God in prayer, and praise Him for all that He has done. Whether your eyes are open or closed, He's listening.

Gratitude changes the pangs of memory
into a tranquil joy.

Dietrich Bonhoeffer

MORE THOUGHTS ABOUT JOY

When I met Christ, I felt that I had swallowed sunshine.

E. Stanley Jones

He wants us to have a faith that does not complain while waiting, but rejoices because we know our times are in His hands—nail-scarred hands that labor for our highest good.

Kay Arthur

Our God is so wonderfully good, and lovely, and blessed in every way that the mere fact of belonging to Him is enough for an untellable fullness of joy!

Hannah Whitall Smith

As Catherine of Siena said, "All the way to heaven is heaven." A joyful end requires a joyful means. Bless the Lord.

Eugene Peterson

A WORD TO THE WISE

Joy begins with a choice—the choice to establish a genuine relationship with God and His Son. Joy does not depend upon your circumstances, but upon your relationship with God.

VERSE 40

Beloved, if God so loved us,
we also ought to love one another.

1 John 4:11 NKJV

LOVE ONE ANOTHER

Genuine love requires patience and perseverance. Sometimes we are sorely tempted to treat love as if it were a sprint (which it is not). Genuine love is always a marathon, and those who expect it to be otherwise will always be disappointed.

Building lasting relationships requires a steadfast determination to endure, and as an example of perfect perseverance, we need look no further than our Savior, Jesus Christ. Jesus finished what He began. Despite the torture He endured, despite the shame of the cross, Jesus was steadfast in His faithfulness to God. We, too, must remain faithful in our relationships, especially during times of transition or hardship.

The next time you are tempted to "give up" on a relationship, ask yourself this question: "What would our Savior do?" When you find the answer to that question, you will know precisely what you should do.

To have fallen in love hints
to our hearts that all of earthly life
is not hopelessly fallen.
Love is the laughter of God.

—

Beth Moore

MORE THOUGHTS ABOUT LOVE

Real love has staying power. Authentic love is tough love. It refuses to look for ways to run away. It always opts for working through.

Charles Swindoll

For love to be true, it sometimes has to be velvet and sometimes it has to be steel.

Charles Stanley

So Jesus came, stripping himself of everything as he came—omnipotence, omniscience, omnipresence—everything except love. "He emptied himself" (Philippians 2:7), emptied himself of everything except love. Love—his only protection, his only weapon, his only method.

E. Stanley Jones

The world does not understand theology or dogma, but it does understand love and sympathy.

D. L. Moody

A WORD TO THE WISE

You should love your neighbor as you love yourself. It's a big job, but with God's help, you can do it.

VERSE 41

*Weeping may endure for a night,
but joy comes in the morning.*

Psalm 30:5 NKJV

BEYOND GRIEF

Grief visits all of us who live long and love deeply. When we lose a loved one, or when we experience any other profound loss, darkness overwhelms us for a while, and it seems as if our purpose for living has vanished. Thankfully, God has other plans.

The Christian faith, as communicated through the words of the Holy Bible, is a healing faith. It offers comfort in times of trouble, courage for our fears, hope instead of hopelessness. For Christians, the grave is not a final resting-place; it is a place of transition. Through the healing words of God's promises, Christians understand that the Lord continues to manifest His plan in good times and bad.

God intends that you have a meaningful, abundant life, but He expects you to do your part in claiming those blessings. So, as you work through your grief, you will find it helpful to utilize all the resources that God has placed along your path. God makes help available, but it's up to you to find it and then to accept it.

If you are experiencing the intense pain of a recent loss, or if you are still mourning a loss from long ago, perhaps you are now ready to begin the next stage of your journey with God. If so, be mindful of this fact: As a wounded survivor, you will have countless opportunities to serve others. And by serving others, you will bring purpose and meaning to the suffering you've endured.

MORE THOUGHTS ABOUT OVERCOMING GRIEF

Despair is always the gateway of faith.

Oswald Chambers

There is no way around suffering. We have to go through it to get to the other side.

Barbara Johnson

You learn your theology most where your sorrows take you.

Martin Luther

God's Word never said we were not to grieve our losses. It says we are not to grieve as those who have no hope (1 Thessalonians 4:13). Big Difference.

Beth Moore

The grace of God is sufficient for all our needs, for every problem and for every difficulty, for every broken heart, and for every human sorrow.

Peter Marshall

To pray much is to knock for Him to whom we pray. This is often done more by groans than speeches, by weeping than by addresses.

St. Augustine

Suffering may be someone's fault or it may not be anyone's fault. But if given to God, our suffering becomes an opportunity to experience the power of God at work in our lives and to give glory to Him.

Anne Graham Lotz

There is no pit so deep that God's love is not deeper still.

Corrie ten Boom

In times of deepest suffering it is the faithful carrying out of ordinary duties that brings the greatest consolation.

Elisabeth Elliot

A WORD TO THE WISE

When you grieve, God remains steadfast . . . and He can comfort you.

VERSE 42

Jesus said to him, "'You shall love the Lord your God with all your heart, with all your soul, and with all your mind.' This is the first and great commandment."

Matthew 22:37-38 NKJV

LOVING GOD

Christ's words are unambiguous: "Love the Lord your God with all your heart and with all your soul and with all your mind." But sometimes, despite our best intentions, we fall short of God's plan for our lives when we become embittered with ourselves, with our neighbors, or most especially with our Creator.

If we are to please God, we must cleanse ourselves of the negative feelings that separate us from others and from Him. In 1 Corinthians 13, we are told that love is the foundation upon which all our relationships are to be built: our relationships with others and our relationship with our Maker.

So today and every day, fill your heart with love; never yield to bitterness; and praise the Son of God who, in His infinite wisdom, made love His greatest commandment.

I love Him because
He first loved me,
and He still does love me,
and He will love me
forever and ever.

—

Bill Bright

MORE THOUGHTS ABOUT LOVING GOD

God has a genuine, passionate affection for each of us and invites us to open our hearts to that love and then return love to Him with deep sincerity.

Bill Hybels

Loving Him means the thankful acceptance of all things that His love has appointed.

Elisabeth Elliot

God is so inconceivably good. He's not looking for perfection. He already saw it in Christ. He's looking for affection.

Beth Moore

Joy is a by-product not of happy circumstances, education or talent, but of a healthy relationship with God and a determination to love Him no matter what.

Barbara Johnson

A WORD TO THE WISE

Because God first loved you, you should love Him. And one way that you demonstrate your love is by obeying Him.

VERSE 43

Be strong and courageous, and do the work.
Do not be afraid or discouraged,
for the Lord God, my God, is with you.

1 Chronicles 28:20 NIV

BEYOND THE FEAR
OF FAILURE

As we consider the uncertainties of the future, we are confronted with a powerful temptation: the temptation to "play it safe." Unwilling to move mountains, we fret over molehills. Unwilling to entertain great hopes for the tomorrow, we focus on the unfairness of the today. Unwilling to trust God completely, we take timid half-steps when God intends that we make giant leaps.

Today, ask God for the courage to step beyond the boundaries of your doubts. Ask Him to guide you to a place where you can realize your full potential—a place where you are freed from the fear of failure. Ask Him to do His part, and promise Him that you will do your part. Don't ask Him to lead you to a "safe" place; ask Him to lead you to the "right" place . . . and remember: those two places are seldom the same.

Do not be one of those who,
rather than risk failure,
never attempt anything.

—

Thomas Merton

More Thoughts About Fear of Failure

There comes a time when we simply have to face the challenges in our lives and stop backing down.

John Eldredge

With each new experience of letting God be in control, we gain courage and reinforcement for daring to do it again and again.

Gloria Gaither

Risk must be taken because the greatest hazard in life is to risk nothing.

John Maxwell

Only a person who dares to risk is free.

Joey Johnson

A Word to the Wise

If you're too afraid of failure, you may not live up to your potential. Remember that failing isn't nearly as bad as failing to try.

VERSE 44

The LORD is gracious and full of compassion,
slow to anger and great in mercy.
The LORD is good to all,
and His tender mercies are over all His works.

Psalm 145:8-9 NKJV

GOD'S MERCY

In Psalm 145, we are taught that God is merciful. His hand offers forgiveness and salvation. God's mercy, like His love, is infinite and everlasting—it knows no boundaries.

Romans 3:23 reminds us of a universal truth: "All have sinned, and come short of the glory of God" (KJV). All of us, even the most righteous among us, are sinners. But despite our imperfections, our merciful Father in heaven offers us salvation through the person of His Son.

As Christians, we have been blessed by a merciful, loving God. Now, it's our turn to share His love and His mercy with a world that needs both. May we accept His gifts and share them with our friends, with our families, and with all the people He chooses to place along our paths.

MORE THOUGHTS ABOUT GOD'S MERCY

Looking back over my life, all I can see is mercy and grace written in large letters everywhere. May God help me have the same kind of heart toward those who wound or offend me.

Jim Cymbala

Is your child learning of the love of God through your love, tenderness, and mercy?

James Dobson

Mercy is an attribute of God, an infinite and inexhaustible energy within the divine nature which disposes God to be actively compassionate.

A. W. Tozer

How happy we are when we realize that He is responsible, that He goes before, that goodness and mercy shall follow us!

Mrs. Charles E. Cowman

We must appropriate the tender mercy of God every day after conversion, or problems quickly develop. We need his grace daily in order to live a righteous life.

Jim Cymbala

Storm the throne of grace and persevere therein, and mercy will come down.

John Wesley

When terrible things happen, there are two choices, and only two: We can trust God, or we can defy Him. We believe that God is God, He's still got the whole world in His hands and knows exactly what He's doing, or we must believe that He is not God and that we are at the awful mercy of mere chance.

Elisabeth Elliot

Trust the past to the mercy of God, the present to his love, and the future to his Providence.

St. Augustine

Angels descending, bring from above, / Echoes of mercy, whispers of love.

Fanny Crosby

A Word to the Wise

God forgives sin when you ask . . . so ask! God stands ready to forgive . . . the next move is yours.

*Blessed is the man who walks not
in the counsel of the ungodly,
nor stands in the path of sinners,
nor sits in the seat of the scornful;
but his delight is in the law of the Lord,
and in His law he meditates day and night.*

Psalm 1:1-2 NKJV

WALKING WITH THE RIGHTEOUS

Peer pressure can be a good thing or a bad thing, depending upon your peers. If your peers encourage you to make integrity a habit—and if they encourage you to follow God's will and to obey His commandments—then you'll experience positive peer pressure, and that's good. But, if you are involved with people who encourage you to do foolish things, you're facing a different kind of peer pressure . . . and you'd better beware. When you feel pressured to do things, or to say things, that lead you away from God, you're aiming straight for trouble.

Are you satisfied to follow that crowd? If so, you may pay a heavy price unless you've picked the right crowd.

And while you're deciding whom to follow, be sure you're determined to follow the One from Galilee, too. Jesus will guide your steps and bless your undertakings if you let Him. Your challenge, of course, is to let Him.

To sum it up, here's your choice: you can choose to please God first (and by doing so, strengthen your character), or you can fall prey to peer pressure. The choice is yours—and so are the consequences.

MORE THOUGHTS ABOUT PEER PRESSURE

Comparison is the root of all feelings of inferiority.

James Dobson

We, as God's people, are not only to stay far away from sin and sinners who would entice us, but we are to be so like our God that we mourn over sin.

Kay Arthur

Do you want to be wise? Choose wise friends.

Charles Swindoll

You will get untold flak for prioritizing God's revealed and present will for your life over man's . . . but, boy, is it worth it.

Beth Moore

When we are set free from the bondage of pleasing others, when we are free from currying others' favor and others' approval—then no one will be able to make us miserable or dissatisfied. And then, if we know we have pleased God, contentment will be our consolation.

Kay Arthur

For better or worse, you will eventually become more and more like the people you associate with. So why not associate with people who make you better, not worse?

Marie T. Freeman

You must never sacrifice your relationship with God for the sake of a relationship with another person.

Charles Stanley

A WORD TO THE WISE

Your world is loaded up with pressures, some good and some bad. Your big challenge is to know the difference and act accordingly.

VERSE 46

Even though I walk through the valley
of the shadow of death, I will fear no evil,
for you are with me;
your rod and your staff, they comfort me.

Psalm 23:4 NIV

TRUST THE SHEPHERD

In the 23rd Psalm, David teaches us that God is like a watchful shepherd caring for His flock. No wonder these verses have provided comfort and hope for generations of believers.

You are precious in the eyes of God. You are His priceless creation, made in His image, and protected by Him. God watches over every step you make and every breath you take, so you need never be afraid. But sometimes, fear has a way of slipping into the minds and hearts of even the most devout believers—and you are no exception.

You know from firsthand experience that life is not always easy. But as a recipient of God's grace, you also know that you are protected by a loving Heavenly Father.

On occasion, you will confront circumstances that trouble you to the very core of your soul. When you are afraid, trust in God. When you are worried, turn your concerns over to Him. When you are anxious, be still and listen for the quiet assurance of God's promises. And then, place your life in His hands. He is your shepherd today and throughout eternity. Trust the Shepherd.

Put your hand into the hand of God.
He gives the calmness and serenity
of heart and soul.

Mrs. Charles E. Cowman

MORE THOUGHTS ABOUT GOD'S COMFORT

We all go through pain and sorrow, but the presence of God, like a warm, comforting blanket, can shield us and protect us, and allow the deep inner joy to surface, even in the most devastating circumstances.

Barbara Johnson

When I am criticized, injured, or afraid, there is a Father who is ready to comfort me.

Max Lucado

When God allows extraordinary trials for His people, He prepares extraordinary comforts for them.

Corrie ten Boom

To know that God rules over all—that there are no accidents in life, that no tactic of Satan or man can ever thwart the will of God—brings divine comfort.

Kay Arthur

A WORD TO THE WISE

God will always comfort you so that you, in turn, can have the strength to comfort others.

*God is our refuge and strength,
a very present help in trouble.*

Psalm 46:1 NKJV

GOD IS OUR REFUGE

The words of Psalm 46:1 promise that God is our refuge, a refuge that we all need. From time to time, all of us face adversity, discouragement, or disappointment. And throughout life, we all must endure life-changing personal losses that leave us breathless. When we do, God stands ready to protect us. Psalm 147 assures us that, "He heals the brokenhearted, and binds their wounds" (v. 3, NIV).

Are you anxious? Take those anxieties to God. Are you troubled? Take your troubles to Him. Does the world seem to be trembling beneath your feet? Seek protection from the One who cannot be moved.

The same God who created the universe stands ready and willing to comfort you and to restore your strength. During life's most difficult days, your Heavenly Father remains steadfast. And, in His own time and according to His master plan, He will heal you if you invite Him into your heart.

The sermon of your life
in tough times ministers
to people more powerfully
than the most eloquent speaker.

—

Bill Bright

MORE THOUGHTS ABOUT TOUGH TIMES

Faith is a strong power, mastering any difficulty in the strength of the Lord who made heaven and earth.

Corrie ten Boom

If all struggles and sufferings were eliminated, the spirit would no more reach maturity than would the child.

Elisabeth Elliot

Measure the size of the obstacles against the size of God.

Beth Moore

Even in the winter, even in the midst of the storm, the sun is still there. Somewhere, up above the clouds, it still shines and warms and pulls at the life buried deep inside the brown branches and frozen earth. The sun is there! Spring will come.

Gloria Gaither

A WORD TO THE WISE

When you experience tough times (and you will), a positive attitude makes a big difference in the way you tackle your problems.

VERSE 48

No one can be a slave of two masters,
since either he will hate one and love the other,
or be devoted to one and despise the other.
You cannot be slaves of God and of money.

Matthew 6:24 Holman CSB

KEEPING MONEY IN PERSPECTIVE

Your money can be used as a blessing to yourself and to your loved ones, but beware: You live in a society that places far too much importance on money and the things that money can buy. God does not. God cares about people, not possessions, and so must you.

Money, in and of itself, is not evil, but worshipping money most certainly is. So today, as you prioritize matters of importance for you and yours, remember that God is almighty, but the dollar is not.

When we worship God, we are blessed. But if we worship "the almighty dollar," we inevitably pay a price for our misplaced priorities—and our punishment inevitably comes sooner rather than later. Our challenge, then, is to keep money in proper perspective which, by the way, is God's perspective.

MORE THOUGHTS ABOUT
KEEPING MONEY IN PERSPECTIVE

Have you prayed about your resources lately? Find out how God wants you to use your time and your money. No matter what it costs, forsake all that is not of God.

Kay Arthur

TITHE! Anyone can honk!

Anonymous

One of the dangers of having a lot of money is that you may be quite satisfied with the kinds of happiness money can give and so fail to realise your need for God. If everything seems to come simply by signing checks, you may forget that you are at every moment totally dependent on God.

C. S. Lewis

Your priorities, passions, goals, and fears are shown clearly in the flow of your money.

Dave Ramsey

Attitude is always God's concern. Christ's statement dealing with the rich young ruler was based on that man's attitude, his motivation, and the purpose behind his money.

Larry Burkett

If a person gets his attitude toward money straight, it will help straighten out almost every other area of his life.

Billy Graham

God is entitled to a portion of our income. Not because he needs it, but because we need to give it.

James Dobson

Everything that we own belongs to God—including money—and He will use it to direct our lives.

Larry Burkett

Servants of God are always more concerned about ministry than money.

Rick Warren

Money is a mirror that, strange as it sounds, reflects our personal weaknesses and strengths with amazing clarity.

Dave Ramsey

A WORD TO THE WISE

The Bible clearly warns us never to fall in love with money.

VERSE 49

Love is patient; love is kind.
Love does not envy; is not boastful; is not conceited;
does not act improperly; is not selfish;
is not provoked; does not keep a record of wrongs;
finds no joy in unrighteousness,
but rejoices in the truth; bears all things,
believes all things, hopes all things,
endures all things.

1 Corinthians 13:4-7 Holman CSB

LOVE IS . . .

Love is a choice. Either you choose to behave lovingly toward others . . . or not; either you behave yourself in ways that enhance your relationships . . . or not. But make no mistake: genuine love requires effort. Simply put, if you wish to build lasting relationships, you must be willing to do your part.

Since the days of Adam and Eve, God has allowed His children to make choices for themselves, and so it is with you. As you interact with family and friends, you have choices to make . . . lots of them. If you choose wisely, you'll be rewarded; if you choose unwisely, you'll bear the consequences.

God does not intend for you to experience mediocre relationships; He created you for far greater things. Building lasting relationships requires compassion, wisdom, empathy, kindness, courtesy, and forgiveness (lots of forgiveness). If that sounds a lot like work, it is—which is perfectly fine with God. Why? Because He knows that you are capable of doing that work, and because He knows that the fruits of your labors will enrich the lives of your loved ones and the lives of generations yet unborn.

Love is a steady wish
for the loved person's ultimate good.

C. S. Lewis

MORE THOUGHTS ABOUT LOVE

It is important to know that you have to work to keep love alive; you have to protect it and maintain it, just like you would a delicate flower.

James Dobson

How do you spell love? When you reach the point where the happiness, security, and development of another person is as much of a driving force to you as your own happiness, security, and development, then you have a mature love. True love is spelled G-I-V-E. It is not based on what you can get, but rooted in what you can give to the other person.

Josh McDowell

Truth becomes hard if it is not softened by love, and love becomes soft if not strengthened by truth.

E. Stanley Jones

A WORD TO THE WISE

The key to successful Christian living lies in your submission to the Spirit of God. If you're a Christian, God has commanded you to love people . . . and it's a commandment that covers both saints and sinners.

VERSE 50

If you have faith as a mustard seed,
you will say to this mountain,
"Move from here to there," and it will move;
and nothing will be impossible for you.

Matthew 17:20 NKJV

MOUNTAIN-MOVING FAITH

Because we live in a demanding world, all of us have mountains to climb and mountains to move. Moving those mountains requires faith.

Are you a mountain mover whose faith is evident for all to see? Or, are you a spiritual shrinking violet? God needs more men and women who are willing to move mountains for His glory and for His kingdom.

Jesus taught His disciples that if they had faith, they could move mountains. You can too. When you place your faith, your trust, indeed your life in the hands of Christ Jesus, you'll be amazed at the marvelous things He can do. So strengthen your faith through praise, through worship, through Bible study, and through prayer. And trust God's plans. With Him, all things are possible, and He stands ready to open a world of possibilities to you . . . if you have faith.

Concentration camp survivor Corrie ten Boom relied on faith during her long months of imprisonment and torture. Later, despite the fact that four of her family members had died in Nazi death camps, Corrie's faith was unshaken. She wrote, "There is no pit so deep that God's love is not deeper still." Christians take note: Genuine faith in God means faith in all circumstances, happy or sad, joyful or tragic.

If your faith is being tested to the point of breaking, remember that your Savior is near. If you reach out to Him in faith, He will give you peace and strength. Reach out today. If you touch even the smallest fragment of the Master's garment, He will make you whole. And then, with no further ado, let the mountain moving begin.

MORE THOUGHTS ABOUT FAITH

Faith is seeing light with the eyes of your heart, when the eyes of your body see only darkness.

Barbara Johnson

Just as our faith strengthens our prayer life, so do our prayers deepen our faith. Let us pray often, starting today, for a deeper, more powerful faith.

Shirley Dobson

Grace calls you to get up, throw off your blanket of helplessness, and to move on through life in faith.

Kay Arthur

There are a lot of things in life that are difficult to understand. Faith allows the soul to go beyond what the eyes can see.

John Maxwell

Faith does not concern itself with the entire journey. One step is enough.

Mrs. Charles E. Cowman

If God chooses to remain silent, faith is content.

Ruth Bell Graham

Nothing is more disastrous than to study faith, analyze faith, make noble resolves of faith, but never actually to make the leap of faith.

Vance Havner

A WORD TO THE WISE

If your faith is strong enough, you and God—working together—can move mountains.

VERSE 51

Heaven and earth will pass away,
but My words will never pass away.

Matthew 24:35 Holman CSB

TRUST GOD'S WORD

Are you a person who trusts God's Word without reservation? Hopefully so, because the Bible is unlike any other book—it is a guidebook for life here on earth and for life eternal.

As a Christian, you are instructed to study God's Holy Word, to trust His Word, to follow its commandments, and to share its Good News with the world. The Psalmist writes, "Your word is a lamp to my feet and a light to my path" (Psalm 119:105 NASB). Is the Bible your lamp? If not, you are depriving yourself of a priceless gift from the Creator.

Vance Havner observed, "It takes calm, thoughtful, prayerful meditation on the Word to extract its deepest nourishment." How true. God's Word can be a roadmap to a place of righteousness and abundance. Make it your roadmap. God's wisdom can be a light to guide your steps. Claim it as your light today, tomorrow, and every day of your life—and then walk confidently in the footsteps of God's only begotten Son.

MORE THOUGHTS ABOUT GOD'S WORD

For whatever life holds for you and your family in the coming days, weave the unfailing fabric of God's Word through your heart and mind. It will hold strong, even if the rest of life unravels.

Gigi Graham Tchividjian

The promises of Scripture are not mere pious hopes or sanctified guesses. They are more than sentimental words to be printed on decorated cards for Sunday School children. They are eternal verities. They are true. There is no perhaps about them.

Peter Marshall

Words fail to express my love for this Holy Book, my gratitude for its author, for His love and goodness. How shall I thank Him for it?

Lottie Moon

God can see clearly no matter how dark or foggy the night is. Trust His Word to guide you safely home.

Lisa Whelchel

I believe the reason so many are failing today is that they have not disciplined themselves to read God's Word consistently, day in and day out, and to apply it to every situation in life.

Kay Arthur

The Bible became a living book and a guide for my life.

Vonette Bright

God has given us all sorts of counsel and direction in His written Word; thank God, we have it written down in black and white.

John Eldredge

Meditating upon His Word will inevitably bring peace of mind, strength of purpose, and power for living.

Bill Bright

A WORD TO THE WISE

On your bookshelf you have God's roadmap for life here on earth and for life eternal. How you choose to use your Bible is, of course, up to you . . . and so are the consequences.

VERSE 52

Go, therefore, and make disciples of all nations,
baptizing them in the name of the Father and
of the Son and of the Holy Spirit, teaching them
to observe everything I have commanded you.
And remember, I am with you always,
to the end of the age.

Matthew 28:19-20 Holman CSB

THE GREAT COMMISSION

Are you a bashful Christian, one who is afraid to speak up for your Savior. Do you leave it up to others to share their testimonies while you stand on the sidelines, reluctant to share yours? Too many of us are slow to obey the last commandment of the risen Christ; we don't do our best to "make disciples of all the nations."

Christ's Great Commission applies to Christians of every generation, including our own. As believers, we are commanded to share the Good News with our families, with our neighbors, and with the world. Jesus invited His disciples to become fishers of men. We, too, must accept the Savior's invitation, and we must do so today. Tomorrow may indeed be too late.

You cannot keep silent
once you have experienced
salvation of Jesus Christ.

—

Warren Wiersbe

MORE THOUGHTS ABOUT
THE GREAT COMMISSION

Our commission is quite specific. We are told to be His witness to all nations. For us, as His disciples, to refuse any part of this commission frustrates the love of Jesus Christ, the Son of God.

Catherine Marshall

Your light is the truth of the Gospel message itself as well as your witness as to who Jesus is and what He has done for you. Don't hide it.

Anne Graham Lotz

There is nothing anybody else can do that can stop God from using us. We can turn everything into a testimony.

Corrie ten Boom

Choose Jesus Christ! Deny yourself, take up the Cross, and follow Him—for the world must be shown. The world must see, in us, a discernible, visible, startling difference.

Elisabeth Elliot

A WORD TO THE WISE

The best day to respond to Christ's Great Commission is this day.

VERSE 53

Therefore, whether you eat or drink,
or whatever you do, do all to the glory of God.

1 Corinthians 10:31 NKJV

HIS PRIORITIES
AND YOUR HEALTH

When it comes to matters of physical, spiritual, and emotional health, Christians possess an infallible guidebook: the Holy Bible. And, when it comes to matters concerning fitness—whether physical, emotional, or spiritual fitness—God's Word can help us establish clear priorities that can guide our steps and our lives.

It's easy to talk about establishing clear priorities for maintaining physical and spiritual health, but it's much more difficult to live according to those priorities. For busy believers living in a demanding world, placing first things first can be difficult indeed. Why? Because so many people are expecting so many things from us!

If you're having trouble prioritizing your day—or if you're having trouble sticking to a plan that enhances your spiritual and physical health—perhaps you've been trying to organize your life according to your own plans, not God's. A better strategy, of course, is to take your daily obligations and place them in the hands of the One who created you. To do so, you must prioritize your day according to God's commandments, and you must seek His will and His wisdom in all matters.

Would you like to embark upon a personal journey to better fitness? If so, you should remind yourself that on every step of that journey, you have a traveling companion: your Heavenly Father. Turn the concerns of this day over to Him—prayerfully, earnestly, and often. And trust Him to give you the strength you need to become the kind of person He wants you to become.

MORE THOUGHTS ABOUT HEALTH

Our primary motivation should not be for more energy or to avoid a heart attack but to please God with our bodies.

Carole Lewis

You can't buy good health at the doctor's office—you've got to earn it for yourself.

Marie T. Freeman

God wants you to give Him your body. Some people do foolish things with their bodies. God wants your body as a holy sacrifice.

Warren Wiersbe

If you want to form a new habit, get to work. If you want to break a bad habit, get on your knees.

Marie T. Freeman

The key to healthy eating is moderation and managing what you eat every day.

John Maxwell

Ultimate healing and the glorification of the body are certainly among the blessings of Calvary for the believing Christian. Immediate healing is not guaranteed.

Warren Wiersbe

People are funny. When they are young, they will spend their health to get wealth. Later, they will gladly pay all they have trying to get their health back.

John Maxwell

A WORD TO THE WISE

God has given you a body, and He's placed you in charge of caring for it. Your body is a temple that should be treated with respect.

VERSE 54

Man does not see what the Lord sees,
for man sees what is visible,
but the Lord sees the heart.

1 Samuel 16:7 Holman CSB

KEEPING UP APPEARANCES

The words of 1 Samuel 16:7 remind us God sees the heart. We human beings, on the other hand, are often far more concerned with outward appearances.

Are you worried about keeping up appearances? And as a result, do you spend too much time, energy, or money on things that are intended to make you look good? If so, you are certainly not alone. Ours is a society that focuses intently upon appearances. We are told time and again that we can't be "too thin or too rich." But in truth, the important things in life have little to do with food, fashion, fame, or fortune.

Today, spend less time trying to please the world and more time trying to please your earthly family and your Father in heaven. Focus on pleasing your God and your loved ones, and don't worry too much about trying to impress the folks you happen to pass on the street. It takes too much energy—and too much life—to keep up appearances. So don't waste your energy or your life.

MORE THOUGHTS ABOUT APPEARANCES

Outside appearances, things like the clothes you wear or the car you drive, are important to other people but totally unimportant to God. Trust God.

Marie T. Freeman

Our ultimate aim in life is not to be healthy, wealthy, prosperous, or problem free. Our ultimate aim in life is to bring glory to God.

Anne Graham Lotz

If the narrative of the Scriptures teaches us anything, from the serpent in the Garden to the carpenter in Nazareth, it teaches us that things are rarely what they seem, that we shouldn't be fooled by appearances.

John Eldredge

Once you loosen up, let yourself be who you are: the wonderful, witty woman whom God will use to encourage and uplift other people.

Barbara Johnson

The single most important element in any human relationship is honesty—with oneself, with God, and with others.

Catherine Marshall

Being loved by Him whose opinion matters most gives us the security to risk loving, too—even loving ourselves.

Gloria Gaither

It is impossible to please everybody. It's not impossible to please God. So try pleasing God.

Jim Gallery

Fashion is an enduring testimony to the fact that we live quite consciously before the eyes of others.

John Eldredge

Those who follow the crowd usually get lost in it.

Rick Warren

A WORD TO THE WISE

How you appear to other people doesn't make much difference, but how you appear to God makes all the difference.

Whoever conceals an offense promotes love,
but whoever gossips about it separates friends.

Proverbs 17:9 Holman CSB

ABOVE AND BEYOND GOSSIP

The Bible clearly tells us that gossip is wrong. But when it comes to the special confidences that you share with your very closest friends, gossip can be disastrous.

The Bible reminds us that "Reckless words pierce like a sword, but the tongue of the wise brings healing" (Proverbs 12:18 NIV). Therefore, if we are to solve more problems than we start, we must measure our words carefully, and we must never betray a confidence. But sometimes even the most thoughtful among us may speak first and think second (with decidedly mixed results).

When we speak too quickly, we may say things that that would be better left unsaid. When we forgo the wonderful opportunity to consider our thoughts before we give voice to them, we're putting ourselves and our relationships in danger.

A far better strategy, of course, is to do the more difficult thing: to think first and to speak next. When we do so, we give ourselves ample time to compose our thoughts and to consult our Creator before we say something that we might soon regret.

When you talk,
choose the very same words
that you would use if Jesus were
looking over your shoulder.
Because He is.

Marie T. Freeman

MORE THOUGHTS ABOUT GOSSIP

The things that we feel most deeply we ought to learn to be silent about, at least until we have talked them over thoroughly with God.

Elisabeth Elliot

It is time that the followers of Jesus revise their language and learn to speak respectfully of non-Christian peoples.

Lottie Moon

If you can't think of something nice to say, keep thinking.

Criswell Freeman

Like dynamite, God's power is only latent power until it is released. You can release God's dynamite power into people's lives and the world through faith, your words, and prayer.

Bill Bright

A WORD TO THE WISE

When talking about other people, use this guideline: don't say something behind someone's back that you wouldn't say to that person directly.

VERSE 56

The sensible see danger and take cover;
the foolish keep going and are punished.

Proverbs 27:12 Holman CSB

PLAN AHEAD . . .
AND WORK HARD

Are you willing to plan for the future—and are you willing to work diligently to accomplish the plans that you've made? The Book of Proverbs teaches that the plans of hardworking people (like you) are rewarded.

If you desire to reap a bountiful harvest from life, you must plan for the future while entrusting the final outcome to God. Then, you must do your part to make the future better (by working dutifully), while acknowledging the sovereignty of God's hands over all affairs, including your own.

Are you in a hurry for success to arrive at your doorstep? Don't be. Instead, work carefully, plan thoughtfully, and wait patiently. Remember that you're not the only one working on your behalf; God, too, is at work. And with Him as your partner, your ultimate success is guaranteed.

You can't start building
a better tomorrow if you wait
till tomorrow to start building.

—

Marie T. Freeman

MORE THOUGHTS ABOUT PLANNING

The only way you can experience abundant life is to surrender your plans to Him.

Charles Stanley

Our problem is that we become too easily enamored with our own plans.

Henry Blackaby

Allow your dreams a place in your prayers and plans. God-given dreams can help you move into the future He is preparing for you.

Barbara Johnson

Plan ahead—it wasn't raining when Noah built the ark.

Anonymous

God has a plan for your life . . . do you?

Criswell Freeman

A WORD TO THE WISE

It isn't that complicated: If you plan your steps carefully, and if you follow your plan conscientiously, you will probably succeed. If you don't, you probably won't.

VERSE 57

I have set before you life and death,
blessing and curse. Choose life so that you
and your descendants may live,
love the Lord your God, obey Him,
and remain faithful to Him.
For He is your life, and He will prolong
your life in the land the Lord swore to give
to your fathers Abraham, Isaac, and Jacob.

Deuteronomy 30:19-20 Holman CSB

MAKING GOOD CHOICES

Life is a series of choices. From the instant we wake in the morning until the moment we nod off to sleep at night, we make countless decisions: decisions about the things we do, decisions about the words we speak, and decisions about the thoughts we choose to think. Simply put, the quality of those decisions determines the quality of our lives.

As believers who have been saved by a loving and merciful God, we have every reason to make wise choices. Yet sometimes, amid the inevitable hustle and bustle of life here on earth, we allow ourselves to behave in ways that we know are displeasing to God. When we do, we forfeit—albeit temporarily—the joy and the peace that we might otherwise experience through Him.

As you consider the next step in your life's journey, take time to consider how many things in this life you can control: your thoughts, your words, your priorities, and your actions, for starters. And then, if you sincerely want to discover God's purpose for your life, make choices that are pleasing to Him. He deserves no less . . . and neither do you.

Every day of our lives we make choices
about how we're going to live that day.

Luci Swindoll

MORE THOUGHTS ABOUT CHOICES

Commitment to His lordship on Easter, at revivals, or even every Sunday is not enough. We must choose this day—and every day—whom we will serve. This deliberate act of the will is the inevitable choice between habitual fellowship and habitual failure.

Beth Moore

No matter how many books you read, no matter how many schools you attend, you're never really wise until you start making wise choices.

Marie T. Freeman

Choices can change our lives profoundly. The choice to mend a broken relationship, to say "yes" to a difficult assignment, to lay aside some important work to play with a child, to visit some forgotten person—these small choices may affect many lives eternally.

Gloria Gaither

A WORD TO THE WISE

Every day you make hundreds of choices . . . and the quality of those choices determines the quality of your day and your life.

VERSE 58

Be sober! Be on the alert!
Your adversary the Devil is prowling around
like a roaring lion,
looking for anyone he can devour.

1 Peter 5:8 Holman CSB

BE ALERT FOR
THE ADVERSARY

Sometimes sin has a way of sneaking up on us. In the beginning, we don't intend to rebel against God—in fact, we don't think much about God at all. We think, instead, about the allure of sin, and we think (quite incorrectly) that sin is "harmless."

If we deny our sins, we allow those sins to flourish. And if we allow sinful behaviors to become habits, we invite certain hardships into our own lives and into the lives of our loved ones.

Sin tears down character. When we yield to the distractions and temptations of this troubled world, we suffer. But God has other intentions, and His plans for our lives do not include sin or denial.

As creatures of free will, we may disobey God whenever we choose, but when we do so, we put ourselves and our loved ones in peril. Why? Because disobedience invites disaster. We cannot sin against God without consequence. We cannot live outside His will without injury. We cannot distance ourselves from God without hardening our hearts. We cannot yield to the ever-tempting distractions of our world and, at the same time, enjoy God's peace.

Sometimes, in a futile attempt to justify our behaviors, we make a distinction between "big" sins and "little" ones. To do so is a mistake of "big" proportions. Sins of all shapes and sizes have the power to do us great harm. And in a world where sin is big business, that's certainly a sobering thought.

We cannot out-sin
God's ability to forgive us.
Beth Moore

MORE THOUGHTS ABOUT SIN

Could it be that the greatest sin is simply not to love the Lord your God with all your heart, mind, soul, and strength?

Anne Graham Lotz

An exalted view of God brings a clear view of sin and a realistic view of self.

Henry Blackaby

Sin is any deed or memory that hampers or binds human personality.

Catherine Marshall

Repentance is a complete surrender of my sinfulness to the only One who can cleanse me from all sin, and that is Jesus Christ.

Elisabeth Elliot

A WORD TO THE WISE

Every day of your life, you will be tempted to rebel against God's teachings. Your job, simply put, is to guard your heart against the darkness as you focus on the light.

VERSE 59

Rejoice always, pray without ceasing,
in everything give thanks;
for this is the will of God in Christ Jesus for you.
1 Thessalonians 5:16-18 NKJV

PRAY OFTEN

Is prayer an integral part of your daily life, or is it a hit-or-miss habit? Do you "pray without ceasing," or is your prayer life an afterthought? Do you regularly pray in the quiet moments of the early morning, or do you bow your head only when others are watching?

As Christians, we are instructed to pray often. But it is important to note that genuine prayer requires much more than bending our knees and closing our eyes. Heartfelt prayer is an attitude of the heart.

If your prayers have become more a matter of habit than a matter of passion, you're robbing yourself of a deeper relationship with God. And how can you rectify this situation? By praying more frequently and more fervently. When you do, God will shower you with His blessings, His grace, and His love.

The quality of your spiritual life will be in direct proportion to the quality of your prayer life: the more you pray, the closer you will feel to God. So today, instead of turning things over in your mind, turn them over to God in prayer. Instead of worrying about your next decision, ask God to lead the way. Don't limit your prayers to the dinner table or the bedside table. Pray constantly about things great and small. God is always listening; it's up to you to do the rest.

MORE THOUGHTS ABOUT PRAYER

What God gives in answer to our prayers will always be the thing we most urgently need, and it will always be sufficient.

Elisabeth Elliot

Your family and friends need your prayers and you need theirs. And God wants to hear those prayers. So what are you waiting for?

Marie T. Freeman

It is well said that neglected prayer is the birthplace of all evil.

C. H. Spurgeon

God says we don't need to be anxious about anything; we just need to pray about everything.

Stormie Omartian

When the Holy Spirit comes to dwell within us, I believe we gain a built-in inclination to take our concerns and needs to the Lord in prayer.

Shirley Dobson

The center of power is not to be found in summit meetings or in peace conferences. It is not in Peking or Washington or the United Nations, but rather where a child of God prays in the power of the Spirit for God's will to be done in her life, in her home, and in the world around her.

Ruth Bell Graham

Those who know God the best are the richest and most powerful in prayer. Little acquaintance with God, and strangeness and coldness to Him, make prayer a rare and feeble thing.

E. M. Bounds

A WORD TO THE WISE

There's no corner of your life that's too unimportant to pray about, so pray about everything.

*Be an example to the believers in word,
in conduct, in love, in spirit, in faith, in purity.*

1 Timothy 4:12 NKJV

BEING THE RIGHT KIND
OF EXAMPLE

Whether we like it or not, all of us are role models. Our friends and family members watch our actions and, as followers of Christ, we are obliged to act accordingly.

What kind of example are you? Are you the kind of person whose life serves as a genuine example of righteousness? Are you someone whose behavior serves as a positive role model for others? Are you the kind of person whose actions, day in and day out, are based upon kindness, faithfulness, and a love for the Lord? If so, you are not only blessed by God, but you are also a powerful force for good in a world that desperately needs positive influences such as yours.

We live in a dangerous, temptation-filled world. That's why you encounter so many opportunities to stray from God's commandments. Resist those temptations! When you do, you'll earn God's blessings, and you'll serve as a positive role model for your family and friends.

Corrie ten Boom advised, "Don't worry about what you do not understand. Worry about what you do understand in the Bible but do not live by." And that's sound advice because our families and friends are watching . . . and so, for that matter, is God.

MORE THOUGHTS ABOUT SETTING THE RIGHT KIND OF EXAMPLE

Among the most joyful people I have known have been some who seem to have had no human reason for joy. The sweet fragrance of Christ has shown through their lives.

Elisabeth Elliot

In serving we uncover the greatest fulfillment within and become a stellar example of a woman who knows and loves Jesus.

Vonette Bright

Integrity of heart is indispensable.

John Calvin

Your life is destined to be an example. The only question is "what kind?"

Marie T. Freeman

Each one of us is God's special work of art. Through us, He teaches and inspires, delights and encourages, informs and uplifts all those who view our lives. God, the master artist, is most concerned about expressing Himself—His thoughts and His intentions—through what He paints in our character . . . . [He] wants to paint a beautiful portrait of His Son in and through your life. A painting like no other in all of time.

Joni Eareckson Tada

We must mirror God's love in the midst of a world full of hatred. We are the mirrors of God's love, so we may show Jesus by our lives.

Corrie ten Boom

There is no way to grow a saint overnight. Character, like the oak tree, does not spring up like a mushroom.

Vance Havner

A WORD TO THE WISE

God wants you to be a positive role model. And that's what you should want, too.

VERSE 61

Now godliness with contentment is great gain.
For we brought nothing into this world,
and it is certain we can carry nothing out.
And having food and clothing,
with these we shall be content.

1 Timothy 6:6-8 NKJV

KEEP IT SIMPLE

You live in a world where simplicity is in short supply. Think for a moment about the complexity of your everyday life and compare it to the lives of your ancestors. Certainly, you are the beneficiary of many technological innovations, but those innovations have a price: in all likelihood, your world is highly complex. Consider the following:

1. From the moment you wake up in the morning until the time you lay your head on the pillow at night, you are the target of an endless stream of advertising information. Each message is intended to grab your attention in order to convince you to purchase things you didn't know you needed (and probably don't!).

2. Essential aspects of your life, including personal matters such as health care, are subject to an ever-increasing flood of rules and regulations.

3. Unless you take firm control of your time and your life, you may be overwhelmed by an ever-increasing tidal wave of complexity that threatens your happiness.

Your Heavenly Father understands the joy of living simply, and so should you. So do yourself a favor: keep your life as simple as possible. Simplicity is, indeed, genius. By simplifying your life, you are destined to improve it.

MORE THOUGHTS ABOUT SIMPLICITY

Prescription for a happier and healthier life: resolve to slow down your pace; learn to say no gracefully; resist the temptation to chase after more pleasure, more hobbies, and more social entanglements.

James Dobson

There is absolutely no evidence that complexity and materialism lead to happiness. On the contrary, there is plenty of evidence that simplicity and spirituality lead to joy, a blessedness that is better than happiness.

Dennis Swanberg

Among the enemies to devotion, none is so harmful as distractions. Whatever excites the curiosity, scatters the thoughts, disquiets the heart, absorbs the interests, or shifts our life focus from the kingdom of God within us to the world around us—that is a distraction; and the world is full of them.

A. W. Tozer

Efficiency is enhanced not by what we accomplish but more often by what we relinquish.

Charles Swindoll

A peaceful heart finds joy in all of life's simple pleasures.

Anonymous

We Christians must simplify our lives or lose untold treasures on earth and in eternity. Modern civilization is so complex as to make the devotional life all but impossible. The need for solitude and quietness was never greater than it is today.

A. W. Tozer

A WORD TO THE WISE

Simplicity and peace are two concepts that are closely related. Complexity and peace are not.

*Draw near to God,
and He will draw near to you.*

James 4:8 Holman CSB

DRAW NEAR TO GOD

If God is everywhere, why does He sometimes seem so far away? The answer to that question, of course, has nothing to do with God and everything to do with us.

When we begin each day on our knees, in praise and worship to Him, God often seems very near indeed. But, if we ignore God's presence or—worse yet—rebel against it altogether, the world in which we live becomes a spiritual wasteland.

Are you tired, discouraged, or fearful? Be comforted because God is with you. Are you confused? Listen to the quiet voice of your Heavenly Father. Are you bitter? Talk with God and seek His guidance. Are you celebrating a great victory? Thank God and praise Him. He is the Giver of all things good.

In whatever condition you find yourself, wherever you are, whether you are happy or sad, victorious or vanquished, troubled or triumphant, celebrate God's presence. And be comforted. God is not just near; He has promised that He is right here, right now. And that's a promise you can depend on.

MORE THOUGHTS ABOUT GOD'S PRESENCE

As God perfects us, He keeps us protected from the pride that might otherwise develop by veiling, to some extent, our progress in our own eyes. The light of the glory of His presence shines two ways: it sheds light on the knowledge of God so that we can learn to see Him more clearly, but it also sheds light on ourselves so that we can see our own sin more clearly.

Beth Moore

If you want to hear God's voice clearly and you are uncertain, then remain in His presence until He changes that uncertainty. Often, much can happen during this waiting for the Lord. Sometimes, He changes pride into humility, doubt into faith and peace.

Corrie ten Boom

Make the least of all that goes and the most of all that comes. Don't regret what is past. Cherish what you have. Look forward to all that is to come. And most important of all, rely moment by moment on Jesus Christ.

Gigi Graham Tchividjian

The next time you hear a baby laugh or see an ocean wave, take note. Pause and listen as His Majesty whispers ever so gently, "I'm here."

Max Lucado

Get into the habit of dealing with God about everything. Unless, in the first waking moment of the day you learn to fling the door wide back and let God in, you will work on a wrong level all day. But, swing the door wide open and pray to your Father in secret, and every public thing will be stamped with the presence of God.

Oswald Chambers

If your heart has grown cold, it is because you have moved away from the fire of His presence.

Beth Moore

God walks with us. He scoops us up in His arms or simply sits with us in silent strength until we cannot avoid the awesome recognition that yes, even now, He is here.

Gloria Gaither

A WORD TO THE WISE

God isn't far away—He's right here, right now. And He's willing to talk to you right here, right now.

VERSE 63

The borrower is servant to the lender.

Proverbs 22:7 NIV

BEWARE OF DEBT

We live in a world that is addicted to debt, but you needn't be. Just because our world revolves around borrowed money doesn't mean that you must do likewise.

If you're already living beyond your means and borrowing to pay for the privilege, then you know that sleepless nights and stress-filled days are the psychological payments that must be extracted from those who buy too much "now" in hopes that they can pay for those things "later." Unfortunately, "later" usually arrives sooner than expected, and that's when the trouble begins.

Whether you're buying a mattress, a microwave, or a Maserati, somebody will probably be willing to sell it to you on credit. But the Bible makes it clear that the instant you become a debtor, you also become a servant to the lender. So if you're trying to decide whether or not to make that next big purchase, remember that when it comes to borrowed money, less is usually more . . . much more.

Getting out of the pit requires
we surround ourselves with
people who love us enough
to support us and lift us up
when we are at our ugliest.

—

Dave Ramsey

More Thoughts About Debt

Having money may not make people happy, but owing money is sure to make them miserable.

John Maxwell

God says that when you borrow, you become a servant of the lender; the lender is established as an authority over the borrower. (Proverbs 22:7)

Larry Burkett

Nobody is going to simplify your life for you. You've got to simplify things for yourself.

Marie T. Freeman

A Word to the Wise

Nothing is more dangerous to your financial health than the undisciplined use of credit. Don't borrow money for things that go down in value, and if you can't use credit cards responsibly, cut them up.

VERSE 64

He did it with all his heart.
So he prospered.

2 Chronicles 31:21 NKJV

PUTTING YOURSELF AND YOUR HEART INTO YOUR WORK

The old adage is both familiar and true: We must pray as if everything depended upon God, but work as if everything depended upon us. Yet sometimes, when we are weary and discouraged, we may allow our worries to sap our energy and our hope. God has other intentions. God intends that we pray for things, and He intends that we be willing to work for the things that we pray for. More importantly, God intends that our work should become His work.

Whether you're in school, home, or in the workplace, your success will depend, in large part, upon the passion that you bring to your work. God has created a world in which diligence is rewarded and sloth is not. So whatever you choose to do, do it with commitment, with excitement, with enthusiasm, and with vigor.

God did not create you for a life of mediocrity; He created you for far greater things. Reaching for greater things usually requires work and lots of it, which is perfectly fine with God. After all, He knows that you're up to the task, and He has big plans for you. Very big plans . . .

Life is too short to spend it
being angry, bored, or dull.

Barbara Johnson

MORE THOUGHTS ABOUT PASSION

Success or failure can be pretty well predicted by the degree to which the heart is fully in it.

John Eldredge

We honor God by asking for great things when they are part of His promise. We dishonor Him and cheat ourselves when we ask for molehills where He has offered mountains.

Vance Havner

One of the great needs in the church today is for every Christian to become enthusiastic about his faith in Jesus Christ.

Billy Graham

Everything you love is what makes a life worth living.

John Eldredge

A WORD TO THE WISE

When you are passionate about your life and your faith . . . great things happen.

VERSE 65

And you shall know the truth,
and the truth shall make you free.

John 8:32 NKJV

TRUTH WITH A CAPITAL T

God is vitally concerned with truth. His Word teaches the truth; His Spirit reveals the truth; His Son leads us to the truth. When we open our hearts to God, and when we allow His Son to rule over our thoughts and our lives, God reveals Himself, and we come to understand the truth about ourselves and the Truth (with a capital T) about God's gift of grace.

The familiar words of John 8:32 remind us that when we come to know God's Truth, we are liberated. Have you been liberated by that Truth? And are you living in accordance with the eternal truths that you find in God's Holy Word? Hopefully so.

Today, as you fulfill the responsibilities that God has placed before you, ask yourself this question: "Do my thoughts and actions bear witness to the ultimate Truth that God has placed in my heart, or am I allowing the pressures of everyday life to overwhelm me?" It's a profound question that deserves an answer . . . now.

MORE THOUGHTS ABOUT TRUTH

Only Jesus Christ is the truth for everyone who has ever been born into the human race, regardless of culture, age, nationality, generation, heritage, gender, color, or language.

Anne Graham Lotz

For Christians, God himself is the only absolute; truth and ethics are rooted in his character.

Charles Colson

We have in Jesus Christ a perfect example of how to put God's truth into practice.

Bill Bright

Having truth decay? Brush up on your Bible!

Anonymous

To worship Him in truth means to worship Him honestly, without hypocrisy, standing open and transparent before Him.

Anne Graham Lotz

Those who walk in truth walk in liberty.

Beth Moore

Having a doctrine pass before the mind is not what the Bible means by knowing the truth. It's only when it reaches down deep into the heart that the truth begins to set us free, just as a key must penetrate a lock to turn it, or as rainfall must saturate the earth down to the roots in order for your garden to grow.

John Eldredge

God will see to it that we understand as much truth as we are willing to obey.

Elisabeth Elliot

If the price of which you shall have a true experience is that of sorrow, buy the truth at that price.

C. H. Spurgeon

A WORD TO THE WISE

Jesus offers you the Truth with a Capital T. How you respond to His Truth will determine the direction—and the destination—of your life.

VERSE 66

Therefore, if anyone is in Christ,
he is a new creation;
old things have passed away;
behold, all things have become new.

2 Corinthians 5:17 NKJV

THE NEW YOU

In 2 Corinthians 5:17, we are told that when a person accepts Christ, he or she becomes a new creation. Have you invited God's Son to reign over your heart and your life? If so, think for a moment about the "old" you, the person you were before you invited Christ into your heart. Now, think about the "new" you, the person you have become since then. Is there a difference between the "old" you and the "new and improved" version? There should be! And that difference should be noticeable not only to you but also to others.

Warren Wiersbe observed, "The greatest miracle of all is the transformation of a lost sinner into a child of God." And Oswald Chambers noted, "If the Spirit of God has transformed you within, you will exhibit Divine characteristics in your life, not good human characteristics.

God's life in us expresses itself as God's life, not as a human life trying to be godly."

When you invited Christ to reign over your heart, you became a new creation through Him. This day offers yet another opportunity to behave yourself like that new creation by serving your Creator and strengthening your character. When you do, God will guide your steps and bless your endeavors today and forever.

MORE THOUGHTS ABOUT CONVERSION

Has he taken over your heart? Perhaps he resides there, but does he preside there?

Vance Havner

Be filled with the Holy Spirit; join a church where the members believe the Bible and know the Lord; seek the fellowship of other Christians; learn and be nourished by God's Word and His many promises. Conversion is not the end of your journey—it is only the beginning.

Corrie ten Boom

Being born again is God's solution to our need for love and life and light.

Anne Graham Lotz

God is not a supernatural interferer; God is the everlasting portion of his people. When a man born from above begins his new life, he meets God at every turn, hears him in every sound, sleeps at his feet, and wakes to find him there.

Oswald Chambers

If we accept His invitation to salvation, we live with Him forever. However, if we do not accept because we refuse His only Son as our Savior, then we exclude ourselves from My Father's House. It's our choice.

Anne Graham Lotz

If you are God's child, you are no longer bound to your past or to what you were. You are a brand new creature in Christ Jesus.

Kay Arthur

A WORD TO THE WISE

Unless you're a radically different person because of your relationship with Jesus, your faith isn't what it could be . . . or should be.

VERSE 67

Give thanks to the Lord, for He is good;
His faithful love endures forever.

Psalm 106:1 Holman CSB

HIS LOVE ENDURES

God's love for you is bigger and better than you can imagine. In fact, God's love is far too big to comprehend (in this lifetime). But this much we know: God loves you so much that He sent His Son Jesus to come to this earth and to die for you. And, when you accepted Jesus into your heart, God gave you a gift that is more precious than gold: the gift of eternal life. Now, precisely because you are a wondrous creation treasured by God, a question presents itself: What will you do in response to God's love? Will you ignore it or embrace it? Will you return it or neglect it? The decision, of course, is yours and yours alone.

When you embrace God's love, you are forever changed. When you embrace God's love, you feel differently about yourself, your neighbors, and your world. When you embrace God's love, you share His message and you obey His commandments.

When you accept the Father's gift of grace, you are blessed here on earth and throughout all eternity. So do yourself a favor right now: accept God's love with open arms and welcome His Son Jesus into your heart. When you do, your life will be changed today, tomorrow, and forever.

Being loved by Him
whose opinion matters most
gives us the security to risk loving, too—
even loving ourselves.

Gloria Gaither

More Thoughts About God's Love

The hope we have in Jesus is the anchor for the soul—
something sure and steadfast, preventing drifting or giving
way, lowered to the depth of God's love.

Franklin Graham

I love Him because He first loved me, and He still does
love me, and He will love me forever and ever.

Bill Bright

I think God knew that the message we sometimes need to
hear today is not what a great and mighty God we serve,
but rather what a tender, loving Father we have, even
when He says no.

Lisa Whelchel

A Word to the Wise

When all else fails, God's love does not. You can always
depend upon God's love . . . and He is always your ultimate
protection.

VERSE 68

*No temptation has overtaken you except
such as is common to man; but God is faithful,
who will not allow you to be tempted beyond
what you are able, but with the temptation
will also make the way of escape,
that you may be able to bear it.*

1 Corinthians 10:13 NKJV

RESISTING TEMPTATION

I t's inevitable: today you will be tempted by somebody
or something—in fact, you will probably be tempted
many times. Why? Because you live in a world that
is filled to the brim with temptations! Some of these
temptations are small; eating a second scoop of ice cream,
for example, is enticing but not very dangerous. Other
temptations, however, are not nearly so harmless.

The devil is working 24/7, and he's causing pain and
heartache in more ways than ever before. We, as believers,
must remain watchful and strong. And the good news is
this: When it comes to fighting Satan, we are never alone.
God is always with us, and He gives us the power to resist
temptation whenever we ask Him to give us strength.

In a letter to believers, Peter offered a stern warning: "Your adversary, the devil, prowls around like a roaring lion, seeking someone to devour" (1 Peter 5:8 NASB). As Christians, we must take that warning seriously, and we must behave accordingly.

It is easier to stay out of temptation
than to get out of it.

Rick Warren

MORE THOUGHTS ABOUT TEMPTATION

In the worst temptations nothing can help us but faith that God's Son has put on flesh, sits at the right hand of the Father, and prays for us. There is no mightier comfort.

Martin Luther

Instant intimacy is one of the leading warning signals of a seduction.

Beth Moore

Lord, what joy to know that Your powers are so much greater than those of the enemy.

Corrie ten Boom

Deception is the enemy's ongoing plan of attack.

Stormie Omartian

Flee temptation without leaving a forwarding address.

Barbara Johnson

A WORD TO THE WISE

Because you live in a temptation-filled world, you must guard your eyes, your thoughts, and your heart—all day, every day.

*But this I say: He who sows sparingly
will also reap sparingly, and he who
sows bountifully will also reap bountifully.
So let each one give as he purposes in his heart,
not grudgingly or of necessity;
for God loves a cheerful giver.*

2 Corinthians 9:6-7 NKJV

GENEROSITY NOW

The thread of generosity is woven—completely and inextricably—into the very fabric of Christ's teachings. As He sent His disciples out to heal the sick and spread God's message of salvation, Jesus offered this guiding principle: "Freely you have received, freely give" (Matthew 10:8 NIV). The principle still applies. If we are to be disciples of Christ, we must give freely of our time, our possessions, and our love.

In 2 Corinthians 9, Paul reminds us that when we sow the seeds of generosity, we reap bountiful rewards in accordance with God's plan for our lives. Thus, we are instructed to give cheerfully and without reservation. So today, make this pledge and keep it: Be a cheerful, generous, courageous giver. The world needs your help, and you need the spiritual rewards that will be yours when you give it.

God does not supply money to satisfy
our every whim and desire.
His promise is to meet our needs
and provide an abundance
so that we can help other people.

Larry Burkett

MORE THOUGHTS ABOUT GENEROSITY

We are never more like God than when we give.

Charles Swindoll

Abundant living means abundant giving.

E. Stanley Jones

When somebody needs a helping hand, he doesn't need it tomorrow or the next day. He needs it now, and that's exactly when you should offer to help. Good deeds, if they are really good, happen sooner rather than later.

Marie T. Freeman

The measure of a life, after all, is not its duration but its donation.

Corrie ten Boom

The happiest and most joyful people are those who give money and serve.

Dave Ramsey

A WORD TO THE WISE

God has given so much to you, and He wants you to share His gifts with others.

VERSE 70

*Should we accept only good from God
and not adversity?*

Job 2:10 Holman CSB

LEARNING THE ART OF ACCEPTANCE

If you're like most people, you like being in control. Period. You want things to happen according to your wishes and according to your timetable. But sometimes, God has other plans . . . and He always has the final word. Job understood the importance of accepting God's sovereignty in good times and bad . . . and so should you.

The American theologian Reinhold Niebuhr composed a profoundly simple verse that came to be known as the Serenity Prayer: "God, grant me the serenity to accept the things I cannot change, the courage to change the things I can, and the wisdom to know the difference." Niebuhr's words are far easier to recite than they are to live by.

Oswald Chambers correctly observed, "Our Lord never asks us to decide for Him; He asks us to yield to Him—a

217

very different matter." These words remind us that even when we cannot understand the workings of God, we must trust Him and accept His will.

Are you embittered by a personal tragedy that you did not deserve and cannot understand? If so, it's time to make peace with life. It's time to forgive others, and, if necessary, to forgive yourself. It's time to accept the unchangeable past, to embrace the priceless present, and to have faith in the promise of tomorrow. It's time to trust God completely. And it's time to reclaim the peace—His peace—that can and should be yours.

So if you've encountered unfortunate circumstances that are beyond your power to control, accept those circumstances . . . and trust God. When you do, you can be comforted in the knowledge that your Creator is both loving and wise, and that He understands His plans perfectly, even when you do not.

Loving Him means the thankful acceptance of all things that His love has appointed.

Elisabeth Elliot

MORE THOUGHTS ABOUT ACCEPTANCE

Tomorrow's job is fathered by today's acceptance. Acceptance of what, at least for the moment, you cannot alter.

Max Lucado

I have held many things in my hands, and I have lost them all; but whatever I have placed in God's hands, that I still possess.

Corrie ten Boom

I am truly grateful that faith enables me to move past the question of "Why?"

Zig Ziglar

Ultimately things work out best for those who make the best of the way things work out.

Barbara Johnson

A WORD TO THE WISE

When you encounter situations that you cannot change, you must learn the wisdom of acceptance . . . and you must learn to trust God.

VERSE 71

But be doers of the word,
and not hearers only, deceiving yourselves.

James 1:22 NKJV

ACTIONS SPEAK LOUDER

The old saying is both familiar and true: actions speak louder than words. And as believers, we must beware: our actions should always give credence to the changes that Christ can make in the lives of those who walk with Him.

God calls upon each of us to act in accordance with His will and with respect for His commandments. If we are to be responsible believers, we must realize that it is never enough simply to hear the instructions of God; we must also live by them. And it is never enough to wait idly by while others do God's work here on earth; we, too, must act. Doing God's work is a responsibility that each of us must bear, and when we do, our loving Heavenly Father rewards our efforts with a bountiful harvest.

Do you seek God's peace and His blessings? Then obey Him. When you're faced with a difficult choice or a powerful temptation, seek God's counsel and trust the counsel He gives. Invite God into your heart and act in accordance with His commandments. When you do, you will be blessed today, tomorrow, and forever.

MORE THOUGHTS ABOUT TAKING ACTION NOW

It's sobering, it's shocking, it's almost beyond belief, but it is 100 percent biblically true: Every one of our actions and attitudes affects God. By His nature He is an expressive God, and He has given us the capability of stirring His heart.

Bill Hybels

From the very moment one feels called to act is born the strength to bear whatever horror one will feel or see. In some inexplicable way, terror loses its overwhelming power when it becomes a task that must be faced.

Emmi Bonhoeffer

Logic will not change an emotion, but action will.

Zig Ziglar

A bird does not know it can fly before it uses its wings. We learn God's love in our hearts as soon as we act upon it.

Corrie ten Boom

We spend our lives dreaming of the future, not realizing that a little of it slips away every day.

Barbara Johnson

The church needs people who are doers of the Word and not just hearers.

Warren Wiersbe

Do noble things, do not dream them all day long.

Charles Kingsley

Paul did one thing. Most of us dabble in forty things. Are you a doer or a dabbler?

Vance Havner

Never fail to do something because you don't feel like it. Sometimes you just have to do it now, and you'll feel like it later.

Marie T. Freeman

A WORD TO THE WISE

Because actions do speak louder than words, it's always a good time to let your actions speak for themselves.

VERSE 72

So then, they are no longer two but one flesh.
Therefore what God has joined together,
let not man separate.

Matthew 19:6 NKJV

ABOUT MARRIAGE

L ove is a journey. A healthy marriage is a lifelong exercise in love, fidelity, trust, understanding, forgiveness, caring, sharing, and encouragement. It requires empathy, tenderness, patience, and perseverance. It is the union of two adults, both of whom are willing to compromise and, when appropriate, to apologize. It requires heaping helpings of common sense, common courtesy, and uncommon caring. A healthy marriage is a joy to behold, an even greater joy to experience . . . and a blessing forever.

The loving relationship between a husband and wife may require the couple to travel together through the dark valleys of disappointment and sorrow, but even on those darkest days, the couple can remain steadfast . . . if they choose to follow God.

When we behave ourselves as obedient servants, we honor the Father and the Son. When we live righteously

223

and according to God's commandments, we build better marriages and better lives. When we obey God, He blesses us in ways that we cannot fully understand. So, as this day unfolds, take every step of your journey with God as your traveling companion. Study His Holy Word. Follow His commandments. Support only those activities that further God's kingdom and your spiritual growth. Be an example of righteous living to your neighbors, to your children, and to your spouse. And make certain that you keep God where He belongs: at the center of all your relationships, including your marriage.

A marriage can't survive forever on leftovers.
It needs to be fed continually,
or it will eventually starve.

John Maxwell

MORE THOUGHTS ABOUT MARRIAGE

Both a good marriage and a bad marriage have moments of struggle, but in a healthy relationship, the husband and wife search for answers and areas of agreement because they love each other.

James Dobson

How committed are you to breaking the ice of prayerlessness so that you and your mate can seek the Lord openly and honestly together, releasing control over your marriage into the capable, trustworthy, but often surprising hands of God?

Stormie Omartian

Nothing bonds me closer to my husband than interceding for him. If I sense my passion waning or my emotions sagging, if I find myself pulling back from the demands of marriage, I pray—for my husband.

Joni Eareckson Tada

A WORD TO THE WISE

The best marriages are built upon mutual trust and a shared faith in God. If your marriage is built upon anything less, then you're building upon a foundation of sand.

VERSE 73

*Blessed are those who hunger
and thirst for righteousness,
because they will be filled.*

Matthew 5:6 Holman CSB

LIVING RIGHTEOUSLY

Matthew 5:6 teaches us that righteous men and women are blessed. Do you sincerely desire to be a righteous person? Are you bound and determined—despite the inevitable temptations and distractions of our modern age—to be an example of godly behavior to your family, to your friends, to your coworkers, and to your community? If so, you must obey God's commandments. There are no shortcuts and no loopholes—to be a faithful Christian, you must be an obedient Christian.

You will never become righteous by accident. You must hunger for righteousness, and you must ask God to guide your steps. When you ask Him for guidance, He will give it. So, when you're faced with a difficult choice or a powerful temptation, seek God's counsel and trust the counsel He gives. Invite God into your heart and live according to His commandments. When you do, you will be blessed today, tomorrow, and forever.

> Holiness has never been
> the driving force of the majority.
> It is, however, mandatory for anyone
> who wants to enter the kingdom.
>
> Elisabeth Elliot

MORE THOUGHTS ABOUT DOING WHAT'S RIGHT

Righteousness not only defines God, but God defines righteousness.

Bill Hybels

Becoming pure is a process of spiritual growth, and taking seriously the confession of sin during prayer time moves that process along, causing us to purge our life of practices that displease God.

Elizabeth George

Impurity is not just a wrong action; impurity is the state of mind and heart and soul which is just the opposite of purity and wholeness.

A. W. Tozer

He doesn't need an abundance of words. He doesn't need a dissertation about your life. He just wants your attention. He wants your heart.

Kathy Troccoli

A WORD TO THE WISE

If you really want to follow Jesus, you must walk as He walked—you must strive to lead a righteous life, despite your imperfections.

VERSE 74

*Therefore humble yourselves under
the mighty hand of God, that He may exalt you
in due time, casting all your care upon Him,
for He cares for you.*

1 Peter 5:6-7 NKJV

HE CARES

It is easy to become overwhelmed by the demands of everyday life, but if you're a faithful follower of the One from Galilee, you need never be overwhelmed. Why? Because God's love is sufficient to meet your needs. Whatever dangers you may face, whatever heartbreaks you must endure, God is with you, and He stands ready to comfort you and to heal you.

The Psalmist writes, "Weeping may endure for a night, but joy comes in the morning" (Psalm 30:5 NKJV). But when we are suffering, the morning may seem very far away. It is not. God promises that He is "near to those who have a broken heart" (Psalm 34:18 NKJV).

If you are experiencing the intense pain of a recent loss, or if you are still mourning a loss from long ago, perhaps you are now ready to begin the next stage of your journey with God. If so, be mindful of this fact: the loving heart of God is sufficient to meet any challenge, including yours.

MORE THOUGHTS ABOUT GOD'S SUPPORT

God's help is near and always available, but it is only given to those who seek it.

Max Lucado

In God's faithfulness lies eternal security.

Corrie ten Boom

We shall find in Christ enough of everything we need— for the body, for the mind, and for the spirit—to do what He wants us to do as long as He wants us to do it.

Vance Havner

We have ample evidence that the Lord is able to guide. The promises cover every imaginable situation. All we need to do is to take the hand he stretches out.

Elisabeth Elliot

God uses our most stumbling, faltering faith-steps as the open door to His doing for us "more than we ask or think."

Catherine Marshall

How delightful a teacher, but gentle a provider, how bountiful a giver is my Father! Praise, praise to Thee, O manifested Most High.

Jim Elliot

God is bigger than your problems. Whatever worries press upon you today, put them in God's hands and leave them there

Billy Graham

Snuggle in God's arms. When you are hurting, when you feel lonely or left out, let Him cradle you, comfort you, reassure you of His all-sufficient power and love.

Kay Arthur

No matter what we are going through, no matter how long the waiting for answers, of one thing we may be sure. God is faithful. He keeps His promises. What He starts, He finishes . . . including His perfect work in us.

Gloria Gaither

A WORD TO THE WISE

If you want God's guidance, ask for it. When you pray for guidance, God will give it.

In the same way faith,
if it doesn't have works, is dead by itself.

James 2:17 Holman CSB

FAITH WITHOUT WORKS DOESN'T WORK

The central message of James' letter is the need for believers to act upon their beliefs. James' instruction is clear: "faith without works is dead." We are saved by our faith in Christ, but salvation does not signal the end of our earthly responsibilities; it marks the true beginning of our work for the Lord.

If your faith in God is strong, you will find yourself drawn toward God's work. You will serve Him, not just with words or prayers, but also with deeds. Because of your faith, you will feel compelled to do God's work—to do it gladly, faithfully, joyfully, and consistently.

Today, redouble your efforts to do God's bidding here on earth. Never have the needs—or the opportunities—been greater.

We are saved by faith alone,
but faith is never alone.

—

John Calvin

MORE THOUGHTS ABOUT GOOD WORKS

No good work is done anywhere without aid from the Father of Lights.

C. S. Lewis

The religion of Jesus Christ has an ethical as well as a doctrinal side.

Lottie Moon

Where there are no good works, there is no faith. If works and love do not blossom forth, it is not genuine faith, the Gospel has not yet gained a foothold, and Christ is not yet rightly known.

Martin Luther

It is faith that saves us, not works, but the faith that saves us always produces works.

C. H. Spurgeon

A WORD TO THE WISE

When your good works speak for themselves, don't interrupt.

VERSE 76

So teach us to number our days,
that we may gain a heart of wisdom.

Psalm 90:12 NKJV

THE GIFT OF LIFE

Life is a glorious gift from God. Treat it that way. This day, like every other, is filled to the brim with opportunities, challenges, and choices. But, no choice that you make is more important than the choice you make concerning God. Today, you will either place Him at the center of your life—or not—and the consequences of that choice have implications that are both temporal and eternal.

Sometimes, we don't intentionally neglect God; we simply allow ourselves to become overwhelmed with the demands of everyday life. And then, without our even realizing it, we gradually drift away from the One we need most. Thankfully, God never drifts away from us. He remains always present, always steadfast, always loving.

As you begin this day, place God and His Son where they belong: in your head, in your prayers, on your lips, and in your heart. And then, with God as your guide and companion, let the journey begin . . .

You have a glorious future
in Christ!
Live every moment
in His power and love.

—

Vonette Bright

More Thoughts About Life

As I contemplate all the sacrifices required in order to live a life that is totally focused on Jesus Christ and His eternal kingdom, the joy seeps out of my heart onto my face in a smile of deep satisfaction.

Anne Graham Lotz

The world has never been stable. Jesus Himself was born into the cruelest and most unstable of worlds. No, we have babies and keep trusting and living because the Resurrection is true! The Resurrection was not just a one-time event in history; it is a principle built into the very fabric of our beings, a fact reverberating from every cell of creation: Life wins! Life wins!

Gloria Gaither

A life lived without reflection can be very superficial and empty.

Elisabeth Elliot

A Word to the Wise

Your life is a priceless opportunity, a gift of incalculable worth. You should thank God for the gift of life . . . and you should use that gift wisely.

VERSE 77

Acquire wisdom—
how much better it is than gold!
And acquire understanding—
it is preferable to silver.

Proverbs 16:16 Holman CSB

ACQUIRING WISDOM

Proverbs 16:16 teaches us that wisdom is more valuable than gold. All of us would like to be wise, but not all of us are willing to do the work that is required to become wise. Wisdom is not like a mushroom; it does not spring up overnight. It is, instead, like an oak tree that starts as a tiny acorn, grows into a sapling, and eventually reaches up to the sky, tall and strong.

To become wise, we must seek God's wisdom and live according to His Word. To become wise, we must seek wisdom with consistency and purpose. To become wise, we must not only learn the lessons of the Christian life, we must also live by them.

Do you seek to live a life of righteousness and wisdom? If so, you must study the ultimate source of wisdom: the Word of God. You must seek out worthy mentors and listen carefully to their advice. You must associate, day in and day out, with godly men and women. Then, as you accumulate wisdom, you must not keep it for yourself; you must, instead, share it with your friends and family members.

But be forewarned: if you sincerely seek to share your hard-earned wisdom with others, your actions must give credence to your words. The best way to share one's wisdom—perhaps the only way—is not by words, but by example.

MORE THOUGHTS ABOUT WISDOM

If we neglect the Bible, we cannot expect to benefit from the wisdom and direction that result from knowing God's Word.

Vonette Bright

Knowledge can be found in books or in school. Wisdom, on the other hand, starts with God . . . and ends there.

Marie T. Freeman

Wisdom is knowledge applied. Head knowledge is useless on the battlefield. Knowledge stamped on the heart makes one wise.

Beth Moore

Don't expect wisdom to come into your life like great chunks of rock on a conveyor belt. Wisdom comes privately from God as a by-product of right decisions, godly reactions, and the application of spiritual principles to daily circumstances.

Charles Swindoll

When you and I are related to Jesus Christ, our strength and wisdom and peace and joy and love and hope may run out, but His life rushes in to keep us filled to the brim. We are showered with blessings, not because of anything we have or have not done, but simply because of Him.

Anne Graham Lotz

This is my song through endless ages: Jesus led me all the way.

Fanny Crosby

A WORD TO THE WISE

God makes His wisdom available to you. Your job is to acknowledge, to understand, and (above all) to use that wisdom.

VERSE 78

*But the fruit of the Spirit is love, joy,
peace, patience, kindness, goodness,
faith, gentleness, self-control.
Against such things there is no law.*

Galatians 5:22-23 Holman CSB

THE FRUITS OF THE SPIRIT

In Galations 5, we are also told that when people live by the Spirit, they will bear "fruit of the Spirit." But what, exactly, is the fruit of the Spirit? It's a way of behaving yourself, a way of treating other people, a way of showing the world what it means to be a Christian. The Bible says, "The fruit of the Spirit is love, joy, peace, patience, kindness, goodness, faith, gentleness, self-control."

Today and every day, will you strive to be patient, joyful, loving, and kind? Will you really try to control yourself? And while you're at it, will you be peaceful, gentle, patient, and faithful? If so, you'll demonstrate to the world that the fruits of the Spirit can make a wonderful difference in the lives of good Christian people—people like you!

The Holy Spirit cannot be
located as a guest in a house.
He invades everything.

—

Oswald Chambers

More Thoughts About
the Fruits of the Spirit

Though we, as Christians, are like Christ, having the first fruits of the Spirit, we are unlike Him, having the remainders of the flesh.

Thomas Watson

Some people have received Christ but have never reached spiritual maturity. We should grow as Christians every day, and we are not completely mature until we live in the presence of Christ.

Billy Graham

The Holy Spirit is like a living and continually flowing fountain in believers. We have the boundless privilege of tapping into that fountain every time we pray.

Shirley Dobson

The more we abide in Christ, the more fruit we bear.

Warren Wiersbe

A Word to the Wise

When you are touched by God, everything changes, including your behavior, your motivations, your thoughts, and your priorities.

243

*Train up a child in the way he should go,
and when he is old he will not depart from it.*

Proverbs 22:6 NKJV

TRAINING OUR CHILDREN

In the 22nd chapter of Proverbs, we are instructed to train our children while they are still young. So, as responsible adults, we want to share God's wisdom with the next generation. But we cannot impart what we don't possess. So it's never enough to talk about God's rules; we must also be willing to live by them. Then, when our words match our deeds, we can teach our children using both proclamations and (more importantly) demonstrations.

When are the best times to teach your youngster? Deuteronomy 6:7 instructs you to teach God's wisdom, "When you sit in your house and when you walk along the road, when you lie down and when you get up" (Holman CSB). In other words, you should be ready to share God's teachings at any time: during regular family gatherings (mealtimes, weekends, holidays, etc.) as well as those unplanned "teachable" moments that seem to pop up from time to time.

Deuteronomy 6:7 also makes it clear that you should teach your child when he lies down (with bedtime stories and prayers) and when he gets up (with morning family devotionals).

At what age should you begin teaching your child? As soon as possible! In fact, many experts believe that a significant portion of a person's character is formed by the tender age of six—so when it comes to teaching, the early years are golden. So, while God's grace can transform a person at any age, wise parents begin teaching their youngsters from the cradle onward.

What lessons can you teach a very young child? The simplest and most profound elements of God's moral order. These lessons include, but are not limited to, such topics as kindness, truthfulness, God's love, the gift of eternal life, and, of course, the New Testament message of Jesus Christ.

Our faithfulness, or lack of it,
will have an overwhelming impact
on the heritage of our children.

Beth Moore

MORE THOUGHTS ABOUT CHILDREN

The balance of affirmation and discipline, freedom and restraint, encouragement and warning is different for each child and season and generation, yet the absolutes of God's Word are necessary and trustworthy at all times.

Gloria Gaither

Children are not casual guests in our home. They have been loaned to us temporarily for the purpose of loving them and instilling a foundation of values on which their future lives will be built.

James Dobson

The only real qualifications that parents need is a sincere and diligent desire to follow God's ways. God knew your strengths and weaknesses when you signed up to be a parent, and He still hired you.

Lisa Whelchel

A WORD TO THE WISE

Taking care of children is demanding, time-consuming, energy-depleting . . . and profoundly rewarding. Don't ever overlook the rewards.

When I was a child, I spoke as a child, I understood as a child, I thought as a child; but when I became a man, I put away childish things.

1 Corinthians 13:11 NKJV

STILL GROWING UP

The journey toward spiritual maturity lasts a lifetime. As Christians, we can and should continue to grow in the love and the knowledge of our Savior as long as we live. Norman Vincent Peale had the following advice for believers of all ages: "Ask the God who made you to keep remaking you." That advice, of course, is perfectly sound, but often ignored.

When we cease to grow, either emotionally or spiritually, we do ourselves a profound disservice. But, if we study God's Word, if we obey His commandments, and if we live in the center of His will, we will not be "stagnant" believers; we will, instead, be growing Christians . . . and that's exactly what God intends for us to be.

Life is a series of choices and decisions. Each day, we make countless decisions that can bring us closer to God . . . or not. When we live according to the principles contained in God's Holy Word, we embark upon a journey of spiritual maturity that results in life abundant and life eternal.

We cannot hope to reach Christian maturity
in any way other than by
yielding ourselves utterly and willingly
to His mighty working.

Hannah Whitall Smith

MORE THOUGHTS ABOUT MATURITY

As God perfects us, He keeps us protected from the pride that might otherwise develop by veiling, to some extent, our progress in our own eyes. The light of the glory of His presence shines two ways: it sheds light on the knowledge of God so that we can learn to see Him more clearly, but it also sheds light on ourselves so that we can see our own sin more clearly.

Beth Moore

Integrity and maturity are two character traits vital to the heart of a leader.

Charles Stanley

Growth in depth and strength and consistency and fruitfulness and ultimately in Christlikeness is only possible when the winds of life are contrary to personal comfort.

Anne Graham Lotz

A WORD TO THE WISE

Maturity means that you make wise choices. Immaturity means that you continue making unwise choices . . . it's as simple as that.

VERSE 81

*Shepherd God's flock among you,
not overseeing out of compulsion but freely,
according to God's will;
not for the money but eagerly.*

1 Peter 5:2 Holman CSB

CHRIST-CENTERED LEADERSHIP

The old saying is familiar and true: imitation is the sincerest form of flattery. As believers, we are called to imitate, as best we can, the carpenter from Galilee. The task of imitating Christ is often difficult and sometimes impossible, but as Christians, we must continue to try.

Our world needs leaders who willingly honor Christ with their words and their deeds, but not necessarily in that order. If you seek to be such a leader, then you must begin by making yourself a worthy example to your family, to your friends, to your church, and to your community. After all, your words of instruction will never ring true unless you yourself are willing to follow them.

Christ-centered leadership is an exercise in service: service to God in heaven and service to His children here on earth. Christ willingly became a servant to His followers, and you must seek to do the same for yours.

Are you the kind of servant-leader whom you would want to follow? If so, congratulations: you are honoring your Savior by imitating Him. And that, of course, is the sincerest form of flattery.

You can never separate
a leader's actions from his character.

John Maxwell

MORE THOUGHTS ABOUT LEADERSHIP

A man ought to live so that everybody knows he is a Christian, and most of all, his family ought to know.

D. L. Moody

A wise leader chooses a variety of gifted individuals. He complements his strengths.

Charles Stanley

What do we Christians chiefly value in our leaders? The answer seems to be not their holiness, but their gifts and skills and resources. The thought that only holy people are likely to be spiritually useful does not loom large in our minds.

J. I. Packer

A true and safe leader is likely to be one who has no desire to lead, but is forced into a position of leadership by inward pressure of the Holy Spirit and the press of external situation.

A. W. Tozer

A WORD TO THE WISE

Our world needs all the good leaders it can get, so don't be afraid to take a leadership role . . . now.

VERSE 82

All bitterness, anger and wrath,
insult and slander must be removed from you,
along with all wickedness.
And be kind and compassionate to one another,
forgiving one another,
just as God also forgave you in Christ.

Ephesians 4:31-32 Holman CSB

BEYOND BITTERNESS

In the fourth chapter of Ephesians, we are warned about the dangers of bitterness, and with good reason. Bitterness is a spiritual sickness. It will consume your soul; it is dangerous to your emotional health. It can destroy you if you let it . . . so don't let it!

If you are caught up in intense feelings of anger or resentment, you know all too well the destructive power of these emotions. How can you rid yourself of these feelings? First, you must prayerfully ask God to cleanse your heart. Then, you must learn to catch yourself whenever thoughts of bitterness or hatred begin to attack you. Your challenge is this: You must learn to resist negative thoughts before they hijack your emotions.

When you learn to direct your thoughts toward more positive (and rational) topics, you'll be protected from the spiritual and emotional consequences of bitterness . . . and you'll be wiser, healthier, and happier, too. So why wait? Defeat destructive bitterness today.

MORE THOUGHTS ABOUT BITTERNESS

Grudges are like hand grenades; it is wise to release them before they destroy you.

Barbara Johnson

Bitterness is a spiritual cancer, a rapidly growing malignancy that can consume your life. Bitterness cannot be ignored but must be healed at the very core, and only Christ can heal bitterness.

Beth Moore

Bitterness only makes suffering worse and closes the spiritual channels through which God can pour His grace.

Warren Wiersbe

Sin is any deed or memory that hampers or binds human personality.

Catherine Marshall

Forgiveness is the key that unlocks the door of resentment and the handcuffs of hate. It is a power that breaks the chains of bitterness and the shackles of selfishness.

Corrie ten Boom

Forgiveness enables you to bury your grudge in icy earth. To put the past behind you. To flush resentment away by being the first to forgive. Forgiveness fashions your future. It is a brave and brash thing to do.

Barbara Johnson

Bitterness is the trap that snares the hunter.

Max Lucado

A heart out of tune, out of sync with God's heart, will produce a life of spiritual barrenness and missed opportunities.

Jim Cymbala

A WORD TO THE WISE

You can never fully enjoy the present if you're bitter about the past. Instead of living in the past, make peace with it . . . and move on.

Do not fear, for I am with you;
do not be afraid, for I am your God.
I will strengthen you; I will help you;
I will hold on to you with My righteous right hand.

Isaiah 41:10 Holman CSB

ABOVE AND BEYOND FEAR

We live in a fear-based world, a world where bad news travels at light speed and good news doesn't. These are troubled times, times when we have legitimate fears for the future of our nation, our world, and our families. But we also have every reason to live courageously. After all, since God has promised to love us and protect us, who—or what—should we fear?

Perhaps you, like countless others, have found your courage tested by the anxieties and fears that are an inevitable part of 21st-century life. If so, let the words of Isaiah 41:10 serve as a reminder that God wants you to think less about your challenges and more about His love. Remember that He is not just near, He is here, and He's ready to help. God will comfort you if you ask Him to. So why not ask? And why not now?

When once we are assured
that God is good,
then there can be nothing
left to fear.

—

Hannah Whitall Smith

More Thoughts About Fear

Whether our fear is absolutely realistic or out of proportion in our minds, our greatest refuge is Jesus Christ.

Luci Swindoll

Courage faces fear and thereby masters it. Cowardice represses fear and is thereby mastered by it.

Martin Luther King, Jr.

Fear and doubt are conquered by a faith that rejoices. And faith can rejoice because the promises of God are as certain as God Himself.

Kay Arthur

Our future may look fearfully intimidating, yet we can look up to the Engineer of the Universe, confident that nothing escapes His attention or slips out of the control of those strong hands.

Elisabeth Elliot

A Word to the Wise

Are you feeling anxious or fearful? If so, trust God to handle those problems that are simply too big for you to solve. Entrust the future—your future—to God.

VERSE 84

*The one who lives with integrity lives securely,
but whoever perverts his ways will be found out.*

Proverbs 10:9 Holman CSB

INTEGRITY MATTERS

Charles Swindoll correctly observed, "Nothing speaks louder or more powerfully than a life of integrity." Godly men and women agree.

Integrity is built slowly over a lifetime. It is the sum of every right decision and every honest word. It is forged on the anvil of honorable work and polished by the twin virtues of honesty and fairness. Integrity is a precious thing—difficult to build but easy to tear down.

As believers in Christ, we must seek to live each day with discipline, honesty, and faith. When we do, at least two things happen: integrity becomes a habit, and God blesses us because of our obedience to Him.

Living a life of integrity isn't always the easiest way, but it is always the right way. God clearly intends that it should be our way, too.

Oswald Chambers, the author of the Christian classic devotional text *My Utmost for His Highest*, advised, "Never support an experience which does not have God as its source, and faith in God as its result." These words serve as a powerful reminder that, as Christians, we are called to walk with God and obey His commandments. But, we live in a world that presents us with countless temptations to stray far from God's path. We Christians, when confronted with sins of any kind, have clear instructions: Walk—or better yet run—in the opposite direction.

It has been said that character is what we are when nobody is watching. How true. When we do things that we know aren't right, we try to hide them from our families and friends. But even if we successfully conceal our sins from the world, we can never conceal our sins from God.

If you sincerely wish to walk with your Creator, follow His commandments. When you do, your character will take care of itself . . . and you won't need to look over your shoulder to see who, besides God, is watching.

Maintaining your integrity
in a world of sham
is no small accomplishment.

Wayne Oates

MORE THOUGHTS ABOUT INTEGRITY

God never called us to naïveté. He called us to integrity. The biblical concept of integrity emphasizes mature innocence not childlike ignorance.

Beth Moore

The single most important element in any human relationship is honesty—with oneself, with God, and with others.

Catherine Marshall

Honesty has a beautiful and refreshing simplicity about it. No ulterior motives. No hidden meanings. As honesty and integrity characterize our lives, there will be no need to manipulate others.

Charles Swindoll

A WORD TO THE WISE

Integrity pays big dividends. Deception creates massive headaches. Behave accordingly.

VERSE 85

*One thing I do, forgetting those things which
are behind and reaching forward to those things
which are ahead, I press toward the goal
for the prize of the upward call
of God in Christ Jesus.*

Philippians 3:13-14 NKJV

MAKING PEACE
WITH YOUR PAST

Because you are human, you may be slow to forget yesterday's disappointments. But, if you sincerely seek to focus your hopes and energies on the future, then you must find ways to accept the past, no matter how difficult it may be to do so.

In the third chapter of Philippians, Paul tells us that he chose to focus on the future, not the past. Have you made peace with your past? If so, congratulations. But, if you are mired in the quicksand of regret, it's time to plan your escape. How can you do so? By accepting what has been and by trusting God for what will be.

So, if you have not yet made peace with the past, today is the day to declare an end to all hostilities. When you do, you can then turn your thoughts to wondrous promises of God and to the glorious future that He has in store for you.

MORE THOUGHTS ABOUT THE PAST

We can't just put our pasts behind us. We've got to put our pasts in front of God.

Beth Moore

Yesterday is just experience but tomorrow is glistening with purpose—and today is the channel leading from one to the other.

Barbara Johnson

The pages of your past cannot be rewritten, but the pages of your tomorrows are blank.

Zig Ziglar

Every time the devil reminds you of your past . . . remind him of his future—and yours!

Anonymous

Whoever you are, whatever your condition or circumstance, whatever your past or problem, Jesus can restore you to wholeness.

Anne Graham Lotz

We set our eyes on the finish line, forgetting the past, and straining toward the mark of spiritual maturity and fruitfulness.

Vonette Bright

Our yesterdays present irreparable things to us; it is true that we have lost opportunities which will never return, but God can transform this destructive anxiety into a constructive thoughtfulness for the future. Let the past sleep, but let it sleep on the bosom of Christ. Leave the Irreparable Past in His hands, and step out into the Irresistible Future with Him.

Oswald Chambers

The wise man gives proper appreciation in his life to his past. He learns to sift the sawdust of heritage in order to find the nuggets that make the current moment have any meaning.

Grady Nutt

A WORD TO THE WISE

The past is past, so don't invest all your energy there. If you're focused on the past, change your focus. If you're living in the past, it's time to stop living there.

VERSE 86

*Therefore, get your minds ready for action,
being self-disciplined, and set your hope
completely on the grace to be brought to you
at the revelation of Jesus Christ.*

1 Peter 1:13 Holman CSB

THE NEED FOR
SELF-DISCIPLINE

God's Word reminds us again and again that our Creator expects us to lead disciplined lives. God doesn't reward laziness, misbehavior, or apathy. To the contrary, He expects us to behave with dignity and discipline. But ours is a world in which dignity and discipline are often in short supply.

We live in a world in which leisure is glorified and indifference is often glamorized. But God has other plans. God gives us talents, and He expects us to use them. But it is not always easy to cultivate those talents. Sometimes, we must invest countless hours (or, in some cases, many years) honing our skills. And that's perfectly okay with God, because He understands that self-discipline is a blessing, not a burden.

Proverbs 23:12 advises: "Apply your heart to discipline And your ears to words of knowledge" (NASB). 2 Peter 1:5-6 teaches, "make every effort to supplement your faith with goodness, goodness with knowledge, knowledge with self-control, self-control with endurance, endurance with godliness" (Holman CSB). Thus, God's Word is clear: we must exercise self-discipline in all matters.

When we pause to consider how much work needs to be done, we realize that self-discipline is not simply a proven way to get ahead; it's also an integral part of God's plan for our lives. If we genuinely seek to be faithful stewards of our time, our talents, and our resources, we must adopt a disciplined approach to life. Otherwise, our talents are wasted and our resources are squandered.

Life's greatest rewards seldom fall into our laps; to the contrary, our greatest accomplishments usually require work, perseverance, and discipline. May we, as disciplined believers, be willing to work the rewards we so earnestly desire.

You can't climb the ladder of life
with your hands in your pockets.

Barbara Johnson

MORE THOUGHTS ABOUT DISCIPLINE

"They that sow bountifully shall reap also bountifully," is as true in spiritual things as in material.

Lottie Moon

Obedience to God is our job. The results of that obedience are God's.

Elisabeth Elliot

Simply stated, self-discipline is obedience to God's Word and willingness to submit everything in life to His will, for His ultimate glory.

John MacArthur

As we make an offering of our work, we find the truth of a principle Jesus taught: Fulfillment is not a goal to achieve, but always the by-product of a sacrifice.

Elisabeth Elliot

A WORD TO THE WISE

If you're a disciplined person, you'll earn big rewards. If you're undisciplined, you won't.

VERSE 87

But when the Helper comes,
whom I shall send to you from the Father,
the Spirit of truth who proceeds from the Father,
He will testify of Me.

John 15:26 NKJV

FILLED WITH
THE HOLY SPIRIT

Are you burdened by the pressures of everyday living? If so, it's time to ease the pressure. How can you do it? By allowing the Holy Spirit to fill you and to do His work in your life.

When you are filled with the Holy Spirit, your words and deeds will reflect a love and devotion to God. When you are filled with the Holy Spirit, the steps of your life's journey are guided by the Creator of the universe. When you allow God's Spirit to work in you and through you, you will be energized and transformed.

So today, take God at His word. He has promised to fill you with His Spirit if you let Him. Let Him. And then stand back in amazement as the Father begins to work miracles in your own life and in the lives of those you love.

God wants to teach us that when
we commit our lives to Him,
He gives us that wonderful teacher,
the Holy Spirit.

—

Gloria Gaither

MORE THOUGHTS ABOUT THE HOLY SPIRIT

It is the primary responsibility of the Holy Spirit to glorify Jesus by making us like Him—in our character, in our commitment, and in our communion with the Father.

Anne Graham Lotz

The Holy Spirit will not come to us in his fullness until we see and assent to his priority—his passion for ministry.

Catherine Marshall

We have given too much attention to methods and to machinery and to resources, and too little to the Source of Power, the filling with the Holy Ghost.

J. Hudson Taylor

The church needs the power and the gifts of the Holy Spirit more now than ever before.

Corrie ten Boom

A WORD TO THE WISE

The Holy Spirit is God in us, providing us with all we need to be effective Christians.

VERSE 88

*On the first day of the week, very early
in the morning, they came to the tomb,
bringing the spices they had prepared.
They found the stone rolled away from the tomb.
They went in but did not find the body
of the Lord Jesus. While they were perplexed about
this, suddenly two men stood by them in dazzling
clothes. So the women were terrified and bowed
down to the ground. "Why are you looking for
the living among the dead?" asked the men.
"He is not here, but He has been resurrected!"*

Luke 24:1-6 Holman CSB

CONSIDERING THE RESURRECTION

When we consider the resurrection of Christ, we marvel at God's power, His love, and His mercy. And if God is for us, what can we possibly have to fear? The answer, of course, is that those who have been saved by our living Savior have absolutely nothing to fear.

As we consider the meaning of Christ's life, His death, and His resurrection, we are reminded that God's most precious gift, His only Son, went to Calvary as a sacrifice for a sinful world. May we, as believers who have been saved by the blood of Christ, trust the promises of our Savior. And may we honor Him with our words, our deeds, our thoughts, and our prayers—not only today but also throughout all eternity.

MORE THOUGHTS ABOUT THE RESURRECTION

The Resurrection is the biggest news in history. CNN ought to put it on Headline News every thirty minutes. It should scream from every headline: Jesus is alive!

Dennis Swanberg

Christ is risen! Hallelujah! / Gladness fills the world today; / From the tomb that could not hold Him, / See, the stone is rolled away!

Fanny Crosby

The Resurrection was a proclamation that Christ had conquered sin, death, and the devil. It guarantees there is life beyond the grave.

Charles Stanley

The resurrection of Jesus Christ is the power of God to change history and to change lives.

Bill Bright

The resurrection of Jesus, the whole alphabet of human hope, the certificate of our Lord's mission from heaven, is the heart of the gospel in all ages.

R. G. Lee

The world has never been stable. Jesus Himself was born into the cruelest and most unstable of worlds. No, we have babies and keep trusting and living because the Resurrection is true! The Resurrection was not just a one-time event in history; it is a principle built into the very fabric of our beings, a fact reverberating from every cell of creation: Life wins! Life wins!

Gloria Gaither

A WORD TO THE WISE

The resurrection of Jesus is the foundation of the Christian faith—and it should be the foundation of your family's faith, too.

*A word fitly spoken is like
apples of gold in settings of silver.*

Proverbs 25:11 NKJV

THE WORDS WE SPEAK

Throughout the Book of Proverbs, we are reminded that the words we speak have great power. If our words are encouraging, we can lift others up; if our words are hurtful, we can hold others back. So, if we hope to solve more problems than we start, we must measure our words carefully.

Sometimes, even the most thoughtful among us speak first and think second (with decidedly mixed results). A far better strategy, of course, is to do the more difficult thing: to think first and to speak next.

Do you seek to be a source of encouragement to others? And, do you seek to be a worthy ambassador for Christ? If so, you must speak words that are worthy of your Savior. So avoid angry outbursts. Refrain from impulsive outpourings. Terminate tantrums. Instead, speak words of encouragement and hope to a world that desperately needs both.

The great test of a man's character
is his tongue.

—

Oswald Chambers

More Thoughts About Speech

A little kindly advice is better than a great deal of scolding.

Fanny Crosby

The best use of life is love. The best expression of love is time. The best time to love is now.

Rick Warren

We will always experience regret when we live for the moment and do not weigh our words and deeds before we give them life.

Lisa Bevere

Part of good communication is listening with the eyes as well as with the ears.

Josh McDowell

Attitude and the spirit in which we communicate are as important as the words we say.

Charles Stanley

A Word to the Wise

You can guard your heart by paying careful attention to the words you speak. So measure your words carefully and prayerfully.

*The one who conceals his sins will not prosper,
but whoever confesses
and renounces them will find mercy.*

Proverbs 28:13 Holman CSB

WHEN YOU MAKE A MISTAKE

Everybody makes mistakes, and so will you. In fact, Winston Churchill once observed, "Success is going from failure to failure without loss of enthusiasm." What was good for Churchill is also good for you. You should expect to make mistakes—plenty of mistakes— but you should not allow those missteps to rob you of the enthusiasm you need to fulfill God's plan for your life.

We are imperfect people living in an imperfect world; mistakes are simply part of the price we pay for being here. But, even though mistakes are an inevitable part of life's journey, repeated mistakes should not be. When we commit the inevitable blunders of life, we must correct them, learn from them, and pray for the wisdom not to repeat them. When we do, our mistakes become lessons, and our lives become adventures in growth, not stagnation.

Have you made a mistake or three? Of course you have. But here's the big question: have you used your mistakes as stumbling blocks or stepping stones? The answer to that question will determine how well you will perform in the workplace and in every other aspect of your life.

MORE THOUGHTS ABOUT MISTAKES

Sin is largely a matter of mistaken priorities. Any sin in us that is cherished, hidden, and not confessed will cut the nerve center of our faith.

Catherine Marshall

Very few things motivate us to give God our undivided attention like being faced with the negative consequences of our decisions.

Charles Stanley

A live body is not one that never gets hurt, but one that can to some extent repair itself. In the same way a Christian is not a man who never goes wrong, but a man who is enabled to repent and pick himself up and begin over again after each stumble—because the Christ-life is inside him, repairing him all the time, enabling him to repeat (in some degree) the kind of voluntary death which Christ himself carried out.

C. S. Lewis

One of the ways God refills us after failure is through the blessing of Christian fellowship. Just experiencing the joy of simple activities shared with other children of God can have a healing effect on us.

Anne Graham Lotz

Mistakes offer the possibility for redemption and a new start in God's kingdom. No matter what you're guilty of, God can restore your innocence.

Barbara Johnson

In essence, my testimony is that there is life after failure: abundant, effective, spirit-filled life for those who are willing to repent hard and work hard.

Beth Moore

Truth will sooner come out of error than from confusion.

Francis Bacon

A WORD TO THE WISE

When you make a mistake, the time to make things better is now, not later! The sooner you address your problem, the better.

VERSE 91

Commit your activities to the Lord
and your plans will be achieved.

Proverbs 16:3 Holman CSB

DEFINING SUCCESS

How do you define success? Do you define it as the accumulation of material possessions or the adulation of your neighbors? If so, you need to reorder your priorities. Genuine success has little to do with fame or fortune; it has everything to do with God's gift of love and His promise of salvation.

If you have accepted Christ as your personal Savior, you are already a towering success in the eyes of God, but there is still more that you can do. Your task—as a believer who has been touched by the Creator's grace—is to accept the spiritual abundance and peace that He offers through the person of His Son. Then, you can share the healing message of God's love and His abundance with a world that desperately needs both. When you do, you have reached the pinnacle of success.

Winners see an answer
for every problem;
losers see a problem
in every answer.

—

Barbara Johnson

MORE THOUGHTS ABOUT SUCCESS

We, as believers, must allow God to define success. And, when we do, God blesses us with His love and His grace.

Jim Gallery

There's not much you can't achieve or endure if you know God is walking by your side. Just remember: Someone knows, and Someone cares.

Bill Hybels

Often, attitude is the only difference between success and failure.

John Maxwell

Success and happiness are not destinations. They are exciting, never-ending journeys.

Zig Ziglar

A WORD TO THE WISE

Don't let the world define success for you. Only God can do that.

VERSE 92

Do you see a man skilled in his work?
He will stand in the presence of kings.

Proverbs 22:29 Holman CSB

SEARCHING FOR EXCELLENCE

How does God intend for us to work? Does He intend for us to work diligently, or does He, instead, reward mediocrity? The answer is obvious. God has created a world in which hard work is rewarded and sloppy work is not. Yet sometimes, we may seek ease over excellence, or we may be tempted to take shortcuts when God intends that we walk the straight and narrow path.

Today, heed God's Word by doing good work. Wherever you find yourself, whatever your job description, do your work, and do it with all your heart. When you do, you will most certainly win the recognition of your peers. But more importantly, God will bless your efforts and use you in ways that only He can understand. So do your work with focus and dedication. And leave the rest up to God.

MORE THOUGHTS ABOUT EXCELLENCE

I lived with Indians who made pots out of clay which they used for cooking. Nobody was interested in the pot. Everybody was interested in what was inside. The same clay taken out of the same riverbed, always made in the same design, nothing special about it. Well, I'm a clay pot, and let me not forget it. But, the excellency of the power is of God and not us.

Elisabeth Elliot

Freedom is not an absence of responsibility; but rather a reward we receive when we've performed our responsibility with excellence.

Charles Swindoll

Praise Him! Praise Him! / Tell of His excellent greatness. / Praise Him! Praise Him! / Ever in joyful song!

Fanny Crosby

Great relief and satisfaction can come from seeking God's priorities for us in each season, discerning what is "best" in the midst of many noble opportunities, and pouring our most excellent energies into those things.

Beth Moore

With the goodness of God to desire our highest welfare and the wisdom of God to plan it, what do we lack? Surely we are the most favored of all creatures.

A. W. Tozer

Few things fire up a person's commitment like dedication to excellence.

John Maxwell

Ordinary work, which is what most of us do most of the time, is ordained by God every bit as much as is the extraordinary.

Elisabeth Elliot

If, in your working hours, you make the work your end, you will presently find yourself all unawares inside the only circle in your profession that really matters. You will be one of the sound craftsmen, and other sound craftsmen will know it.

C. S. Lewis

A WORD TO THE WISE

Excellence is habit-forming, so give your best every time you go to work.

So he who had received five talents came and
brought five other talents, saying,
"Lord, you delivered to me five talents;
look, I have gained five more talents besides them."
His lord said to him, "Well done, good and
faithful servant; you were faithful over a few things,
I will make you ruler over many things.
Enter into the joy of your lord."

Matthew 25:20-21 NKJV

USING YOUR TALENTS

The old saying is both familiar and true: "What we are is God's gift to us; what we become is our gift to God." Each of us possesses special talents, gifted by God, that can be nurtured carefully or ignored totally. Our challenge, of course, is to use our abilities to the greatest extent possible and to use them in ways that honor our Savior.

Are you using your natural talents to make God's world a better place? If so, congratulations. But if you have gifts that you have not fully explored and developed, perhaps you need to have a chat with the One who gave you those gifts in the first place. Your talents are priceless treasures offered from your Heavenly Father. Use them. After all, an obvious way to say "thank You" to the Giver is to use the gifts He has given.

In the great orchestra we call life,
you have an instrument and a song,
and you owe it to God
to play them both sublimely.

Max Lucado

MORE THOUGHTS ABOUT TALENTS

Not everyone possesses boundless energy or a conspicuous talent. We are not equally blessed with great intellect or physical beauty or emotional strength. But we have all been given the same ability to be faithful.

Gigi Graham Tchividjian

You are a unique blend of talents, skills, and gifts, which makes you an indispensable member of the body of Christ.

Charles Stanley

God often reveals His direction for our lives through the way He made us . . . with a certain personality and unique skills.

Bill Hybels

A WORD TO THE WISE

God has given you a unique array of talents and opportunities. The rest is up to you.

VERSE 94

Pride goes before destruction,
and a haughty spirit before a fall.
Proverbs 16:18 NKJV

BEWARE OF PRIDE

The words from Proverbs 16 remind us that pride and destruction are traveling partners. But as imperfect human beings, we are tempted to puff out our chests and crow about our own accomplishments. When we do so, we delude ourselves.

As Christians, we have a profound reason to be humble: We have been refashioned and saved by Jesus Christ, and that salvation came not because of our own good works but because of God's grace. Thus, we are not "self-made"; we are "God-made" and "Christ-saved." How, then, can we be boastful? The answer, of course, is simple: if we are honest with ourselves and with our God, we cannot be boastful. In the quiet moments, when we search the depths of our own hearts, we know that whatever "it" is, God did that. And He deserves the credit.

Jesus had a humble heart.
If He abides in us,
pride will never
dominate our lives.

—

Billy Graham

MORE THOUGHTS ABOUT PRIDE

That's what I love about serving God. In His eyes, there are no little people . . . because there are no big people. We are all on the same playing field. We all start at square one. No one has it better than the other, or possesses unfair advantage.

Joni Eareckson Tada

There is nothing so natural to man, nothing so insidious and hidden from our sight, nothing so difficult and dangerous, as pride.

Andrew Murray

All kindness and good deeds, we must keep silent. The result will be an inner reservoir of personal power.

Catherine Marshall

Our Lord did not say it was wrong to pray in the corners of the street, but he did say it was wrong to have the motive to "be seen of men."

Oswald Chambers

A WORD TO THE WISE

All of your talents and abilities come from God. Give Him thanks, and give Him the glory.

If we confess our sins,
He is faithful and righteous to forgive us
our sins and to cleanse us
from all unrighteousness.

1 John 1:9 Holman CSB

REAL REPENTANCE

Who among us has sinned? All of us. But, God calls upon us to turn away from sin by following His commandments. And the good news is this: When we do ask God's forgiveness and turn our hearts to Him, He forgives us absolutely and completely.

Genuine repentance requires more than simply offering God apologies for our misdeeds. Real repentance may start with feelings of sorrow and remorse, but it ends only when we turn away from the sin that has heretofore distanced us from our Creator. In truth, we offer our most meaningful apologies to God not with our words, but with our actions. As long as we are still engaged in sin, we may be "repenting," but we have not fully "repented."

Is there an aspect of your life that is distancing you from your God? If so, ask for His forgiveness, and—just as importantly—stop sinning. Then, wrap yourself in the protection of God's Word. When you do, you will be secure.

Real repentance is always accompanied
by godly sorrow.
Asking God to forgive us for a sin
we are not yet sorry we committed
is a waste of time.

Beth Moore

MORE THOUGHTS ABOUT REPENTANCE

Four marks of true repentance are: acknowledgement of wrong, willingness to confess it, willingness to abandon it, and willingness to make restitution.

Corrie ten Boom

The pardon of God deletes past, present, and future sins—completely!

Franklin Graham

Repentance is among other things a sincere apology to God for distrusting Him so long, and faith is throwing oneself upon Christ in complete confidence.

A. W. Tozer

Full and true repentance is literally an about-face. It means turning completely around, away from sin, and turning toward God.

Shirley Dobson

A WORD TO THE WISE

If you're engaged in behavior that is displeasing to God, repent today—tomorrow may be too late.

In fact, when we were with you,
this is what we commanded you:
"If anyone isn't willing to work, he should not eat."

2 Thessalonians 3:10 Holman CSB

WE'RE EXPECTED TO WORK

God's Word teaches us the value of hard work. In his second letter to the Thessalonians, Paul warns, "If anyone isn't willing to work, he should not eat." And the Book of Proverbs proclaims, "One who is slack in his work is brother to one who destroys" (18:9 NIV). In short, God has created a world in which diligence is rewarded but sloth is not. So, whatever it is that you choose to do, do it with commitment, excitement, and vigor.

Hard work is not simply a proven way to get ahead; it's also part of God's plan for you. God did not create you for a life of mediocrity; He created you for far greater things. Reaching for greater things usually requires work and lots of it, which is perfectly fine with God. After all, He knows that you're up to the task, and He has big plans for you if you possess a loving heart and willing hands.

MORE THOUGHTS ABOUT WORK

Thank God every morning when you get up that you have something which must be done, whether you like it or not. Work breeds a hundred virtues that idleness never knows.

Charles Kingsley

You can't climb the ladder of life with your hands in your pockets.

Barbara Johnson

We must trust as if it all depended on God and work as if it all depended on us.

C. H. Spurgeon

Great relief and satisfaction can come from seeking God's priorities for us in each season, discerning what is "best" in the midst of many noble opportunities, and pouring our most excellent energies into those things.

Beth Moore

The world does not consider labor a blessing, therefore it flees and hates it, but the pious who fear the Lord labor with a ready and cheerful heart, for they know God's command, and they acknowledge His calling.

Martin Luther

In the very place where God has put us, whatever its limitations, whatever kind of work it may be, we may indeed serve the Lord Christ.

Elisabeth Elliot

If you honor God with your work, He will honor you because of your work.

Marie T. Freeman

It may be that the day of judgment will dawn tomorrow; in that case, we shall gladly stop working for a better tomorrow. But not before.

Dietrich Bonhoeffer

Few things fire up a person's commitment like dedication to excellence.

John Maxwell

A WORD TO THE WISE

When you find work that pleases God—and when you apply yourself conscientiously to the job at hand—you'll be rewarded.

*Do not love the world
or the things in the world.
If anyone loves the world,
the love of the Father is not in him.*

1 John 2:15 NKJV

THE WORLD'S TREASURES OR GOD'S TREASURES?

All of mankind is engaged in a colossal, worldwide treasure hunt. Some folks seek treasure from earthly sources, treasures such as material wealth or public acclaim; others seek God's treasures by making Him the cornerstone of their lives.

What kind of treasure hunter are you? Are you so caught up in the demands of popular society that you sometimes allow the search for worldly treasures to become your primary focus? If so, it's time to reorganize your daily to-do list by placing God in His rightful place: first place.

If you sincerely seek to strengthen your character, you'll focus more intently on God's treasures and less intently on the world's treasures. Don't allow anyone or anything to separate you from your Heavenly Father and His only begotten Son.

Society's priorities are transitory; God's priorities are permanent. The world's treasures are difficult to find and difficult to keep; God's treasures are ever-present and everlasting. Which treasures and whose priorities will you claim as your own? The answer should be obvious.

MORE THOUGHTS ABOUT WORLDLINESS

Our fight is not against any physical enemy; it is against organizations and powers that are spiritual. We must struggle against sin all our lives, but we are assured we will win.

Corrie ten Boom

Every day, I find countless opportunities to decide whether I will obey God and demonstrate my love for Him or try to please myself or the world system. God is waiting for my choices.

Bill Bright

The true Christian, though he is in revolt against the world's efforts to brainwash him, is no mere rebel for rebellion's sake. He dissents from the world because he knows that it cannot make good on its promises.

A. W. Tozer

All those who look to draw their satisfaction from the wells of the world—pleasure, popularity, position, possessions, politics, power, prestige, finances, family, friends, fame, fortune, career, children, church, clubs, sports, sex, success, recognition, reputation, religion, education, entertainment, exercise, honors, health, hobbies—will soon be thirsty again!

Anne Graham Lotz

As we have by faith said no to sin, so we should by faith say yes to God and set our minds on things above, where Christ is seated in the heavenlies.

Vonette Bright

He who dies with the most toys . . . still dies.

Anonymous

A WORD TO THE WISE

The world is designed to distract you—and distance you—from your faith. So you must guard yourself against these distractions . . . or face the consequences.

VERSE 98

For I am the Lord, I do not change.

Malachi 3:6 NKJV

HE DOES NOT CHANGE

Our world is in a state of constant change. God is not. At times, the world seems to be trembling beneath our feet. But we can be comforted in the knowledge that our Heavenly Father is the rock that cannot be shaken. His Word promises, "I am the Lord, I do not change."

Every day that we live, we mortals encounter a multitude of changes—some good, some not so good. And on occasion, all of us must endure life-changing personal losses that leave us heartbroken. When we do, our Heavenly Father stands ready to comfort us, to guide us, and—in time—to heal us.

Is the world spinning a little too fast for your liking? Are you facing difficult circumstances or unwelcome changes? If so, please remember that God is far bigger than any problem you may face. So, instead of worrying about life's inevitable challenges, put your faith in the Father and His only begotten Son. After all, "Jesus Christ is the same yesterday, today, and forever" (Hebrews 13:8 NKJV).

And it is precisely because your Savior does not change that you can face your challenges with courage for today and hope for tomorrow.

Are you anxious about situations that you cannot control? Take your anxieties to God. Are you troubled? Take your troubles to Him. Does your little corner of the universe seem to be trembling beneath your feet? Seek protection from the One who cannot be moved. The same God who created the universe will protect you if you ask Him . . . so ask Him . . . and then serve Him with willing hands and a trusting heart.

To God be the glory,
great things He has done;
So loved He the world
that He gave us His Son.

Fanny Crosby

MORE THOUGHTS ABOUT GOD

God does not tell us what He is going to do; He reveals to us who He is.

Oswald Chambers

God is the beyond in the midst of our life.

Dietrich Bonhoeffer

When all else is gone, God is still left. Nothing changes Him.

Hannah Whitall Smith

God's actual divine essence and his will are absolutely beyond all human thought, human understanding or wisdom; in short, they are and ever will be incomprehensible, inscrutable, and altogether hidden to human reason.

Martin Luther

A WORD TO THE WISE

Because God is infinite and eternal, you cannot comprehend Him. But you can understand your need to praise Him, to love Him, and to obey His Word.

You are the light of the world.
A city that is set on a hill cannot be hidden.
Nor do they light a lamp and put it under a basket,
but on a lampstand, and it gives light to all
who are in the house.
Let your light so shine before men,
that they may see your good works
and glorify your Father in heaven.

Matthew 5:14-16 NKJV

YOU ARE THE LIGHT

Matthew 5:14-16 makes it clear: Because you are a Christian, you are indeed "the light of the world." The Bible also says that you should live in a way that lets other people understand what it means to be a follower of Jesus.

Your personal testimony is profoundly important, but perhaps because of shyness (or because of the fear of being rebuffed), you've been hesitant to share your experiences. If so, you should start paying less attention to your own insecurities and more attention to the message that God wants you to share with the world.

Corrie ten Boom observed, "There is nothing anybody else can do that can stop God from using us. We can turn everything into a testimony." Her words remind us that when we speak up for God, our actions may speak even more loudly than our words.

When we let other people know the details of our faith, we assume an important responsibility: the responsibility of making certain that our words are reinforced by our actions. When we share our testimonies, we must also be willing to serve as shining examples of righteousness—undeniable examples of the changes that Jesus makes in the lives of those who accept Him as their Savior.

Are you willing to follow in the footsteps of Jesus? If so, you must also be willing to talk about Him. And make no mistake—the time to express your belief in Him is now. You know how He has touched your own heart; help Him do the same for others.

God has ordained that others may see
the reality of His presence by
the illumination our lives shed forth.

Beth Moore

MORE THOUGHTS ABOUT WITNESSING

Stay on the issue of Christ when witnessing, not the church, or denominations, or religion, or theological differences, or doctrinal questions. Speak precisely of Jesus, the Savior.

Charles Swindoll

When Christians live out their faith with authenticity and boldness, they put a little zing into a sometimes bland cup of soup. They catch people off guard and make them wince. They wake people up with their challenges and seemingly radical points of view. And, they overturn a few applecarts here and there.

Bill Hybels

In your desire to share the gospel, you may be the only Jesus someone else will ever meet. Be real and be involved with people.

Barbara Johnson

A WORD TO THE WISE

Whether you realize it or not, you have a profound responsibility to tell as many people as you can about the eternal life that Christ offers to those who believe in Him.

VERSE 100

I was glad when they said unto me,
Let us go into the house of the LORD.

Psalm 122:1 KJV

OUR NEED
TO WORSHIP GOD

All of humanity is engaged in worship. The question is not whether we worship, but what we worship. Wise men and women choose to worship God. When they do, they are blessed with a plentiful harvest of joy, peace, and abundance. Other people choose to distance themselves from God by foolishly worshipping things that are intended to bring personal gratification but not spiritual gratification. Such choices often have tragic consequences.

If we place our love for material possessions above our love for God—or if we yield to the countless temptations of this world—we find ourselves engaged in a struggle between good and evil, a clash between God and Satan. Our responses to these struggles have implications that echo throughout our families and throughout our communities.

How can we ensure that we cast our lot with God? We do so, in part, by the practice of regular, purposeful worship in the company of fellow believers. When we worship God faithfully and fervently, we are blessed. When we fail to worship God, for whatever reason, we forfeit the spiritual gifts that He intends for us.

We must worship our Heavenly Father, not just with our words, but also with deeds. We must honor Him, praise Him, and obey Him. As we seek to find purpose and meaning for our lives, we must first seek His purpose and His will. For believers, God comes first. Always first.

Do you place a high value on the practice of worship? Hopefully so. After all, every day provides countless opportunities to put God where He belongs: at the very center of your life. It's up to you to worship God seven days a week; anything less is simply not enough.

Worship is spiritual.
Our worship must be more than just
outward expression,
it must also take place in our spirits.

Franklin Graham

MORE THOUGHTS ABOUT WORSHIP

Each time, before you intercede, be quiet first and worship God in His glory. Think of what He can do and how He delights to hear the prayers of His redeemed people. Think of your place and privilege in Christ, and expect great things!

Andrew Murray

I am of the opinion that we should not be concerned about working for God until we have learned the meaning and delight of worshipping Him.

A. W. Tozer

In Biblical worship you do not find the repetition of a phrase; instead, you find the worshippers rehearsing the character of God and His ways, reminding Him of His faithfulness and His wonderful promises.

Kay Arthur

A WORD TO THE WISE

When you worship God with a sincere heart, He will guide your steps and bless your life.

It's helpful to commit key Bible verses to memory. On the pages that follow, jot down your own notes about the verses you intend to memorize.

TIPS FOR MEMORIZING BIBLE VERSES

As you memorize Bible verses, here are some things to consider:

1. It helps to write each verse on a note card and carry it with you throughout the week, reviewing the verse often.

2. Memorization is, at its core, the process of moving things from short-term memory into long-term memory. You achieve this through repetition, which means that the more you recite the verse to yourself, the more quickly you'll learn it.

3. Even after you've memorized a particular verse, it's important to review it again and again throughout the year. Otherwise, a verse you've memorized in January may become little more than a foggy recollection by December.

4. Don't be too hard on yourself. If you can't quite master a particular verse, don't quit and don't lose hope. Instead of berating yourself, just keep reciting the verse over and over, until you finally send it into your long-term memory banks.